Praise for

Making Peace with Your Father

Dave Stoop has created a great tool for all who
struggle with the father wound.

Stephen Arterburn

AUTHOR, *EVERY MAN'S BATTLE* AND *TAKE YOUR LIFE BACK*
FOUNDER AND CEO, NEW LIFE MINISTRIES

Here is a book that everyone will want to read.
"Amazingly insightful" and "practical" are descriptive
words that come to mind. Also, the way this resource
is structured gives readers the ability to
immediately find their area of interest.

H. Norman Wright

AUTHOR, *ALWAYS DADDY'S GIRL*
THERAPIST

Making Peace with Your Father does a masterful job of helping us understand the crucial role of our fathers in our overall development. Whether they were active or absent, our fathers played a vital role in shaping who we are. For many, Dad's influence was a painful one. Dr. Stoop offers help and hope by providing specific ways to make peace with our fathers by healing the wounds of the past and pointing the way toward a loving relationship with our heavenly Father. I highly recommend this book.

Mark E. Crawford

AUTHOR, *THE OBSESSIVE-COMPULSIVE TRAP* AND "THE IMPORTANCE OF FATHER,"
A CHAPTER IN *THE COMPLETE CHRISTIAN PARENTING BOOK*
LICENSED PSYCHOLOGIST

In more than 25 years of working with men, I've found one of the biggest roadblocks to becoming whole and healthy is dealing with the deep wounds and hurts from their relationship with their dad. In *Making Peace with Your Father,* Dr. Dave Stoop has given us a practical and invaluable resource that addresses those issues and provides solutions. Whether you need help in dealing with pain from your past or you just want to be a better dad to your own children, you will find wisdom and encouragement here. Reading just the chapter on steps toward hope and healing is worth the price of the book.

Gary. J Oliver, Ph.D.

COAUTHOR, *RAISING SONS AND LOVING IT*
EXECUTIVE DIRECTOR, THE CENTER FOR MARRIAGE AND FAMILY STUDIES
PROFESSOR OF PSYCHOLOGY AND THEOLOGY, JOHN BROWN UNIVERSITY
MEMBER OF THE BOARD OF DIRECTORS, PROMISE KEEPERS

Making Peace

With Your

Father

DAVID STOOP, PH.D.

Revell

a division of Baker Publishing Group
Grand Rapids, Michigan

© 1992, 2004 by David Stoop

Published by Revell
a division of Baker Publishing Group
PO Box 6287, Grand Rapids, MI 49516-6287
www.revellbooks.com

Special Ministry edition published 2018
ISBN 978-0-8007-3526-5

Previously published by Revell Books and Regal Books

Making Peace with Your Father was originally published by Tyndale House Publishers in 1992.

Printed in the United States of America

The Library of Congress has cataloged the original edition as follows:
   Stoop, David A.
     Making peace with your father / David Stoop.— Rev. and updated ed.
        p. cm.
     ISBN 0-8307-3441-4
     1. Fathers. 2. Father and child. 3. Interpersonal relations.
   I. Title.
   HQ756.S84 2004
   306.874'2—dc22   2003026263

All Scripture quotations, unless otherwise noted, are from The Living Bible, copyright © 1971. Used by permission of Tyndale House Publishers, Inc., Wheaton, Illinois 60189. All rights reserved.

Scripture quotations labeled KJV are from the King James Version of the Bible.

Scripture quotations labeled NIV are from the Holy Bible, New International Version®. NIV®. Copyright © 1973, 1978, 1984 by Biblica, Inc.™ Used by permission of Zondervan. All rights reserved worldwide. www.zondervan.com

Scripture quotations labeled PHILLIPS are from The New Testament in Modern English, revised edition—J. B. Phillips, translator. © J. B. Phillips 1958, 1960, 1972. Used by permission of Macmillan Publishing Co., Inc.

Published in association with the literary agency of Alive Communications, Inc., 7680 Goddard Street, Suite 200, Colorado Springs, CO 80920.

To my sons
Mike, Greg, and Eric

Contents

Part One
The Importance of Father

The Competitive Father
The Idealized Father
The Good-Enough Father

The Physically Abusive Father
The Molesting Father
The Terrorizing Father
The Weak Father

Part Four
Hope and Healing

Step One: Identify the Symptoms
Step Two: Get the Facts
Step Three: Identify Family Secrets and Family Myths
Step Four: Speak the Unspoken
Step Five: Rewrite History
Step Six: Process the Losses

Step Seven: Wait
Step Eight: Forgive
Step Nine: Invite Others to Share Your Journey
Step Ten: Explore New Roles
Step Eleven: Redeem the Past

Part One

The Importance of Father

Which of us has looked into his father's heart?
Thomas Wolfe, *Look Homeward Angel*

ONE

The Journey Toward Dad

Fathers. Everyone has one—for better or for worse. And everyone needs a daddy.

What was your father like? When you think about your father do you remember warm and happy times? Wrestling on the living room floor, listening to his fanciful stories at bedtime, sneaking off for an ice cream treat, talking about your day at school?

Or do you have darker memories? Being yelled at for spilling your milk, smacked on the side of the head for asking a question during his favorite TV program, humiliated in front of your friends because you struck out in the crucial ninth inning?

Do you perhaps have few or no memories of Father, because he was seldom or never present in your life?

Whether your memories are positive or negative, whether your father was present or absent, he has shaped and continues to shape who you are today. Every year many clients come to our clinic for counseling about a variety of issues. Often we find that these clients need to discuss and resolve some very painful father issues before we can deal with what appears to be the "real" problem.

As we shall see in this book, fathers play a crucial role in child development. To put it more pointedly: Our fathers, yours and mine, have played a major role in making us who we are today. Their successes have strengthened us, their failures have weakened us.

Making peace with Father—it's a journey as well as a destination. When you picked up this book, you began the journey. The book may not take long to read; the journey can last a lifetime.

As you make the journey, you will have moments of excruciating pain. You will also feel more joy than you ever dreamed possible.

You will open old wounds, but you will also find healing.

At times you will wonder if you will ever find what or whom you are seeking. Then hope will break through and you will be filled with the courage to continue.

The journey toward Dad is a perilous but necessary voyage. We all must take it, if we want to be whole.

It is a journey I have made and am still making. I would like to invite you to make this journey with me.

My own journey goes back fifty years.

Life with Father

When I was a boy, about all we expected of Dad was that he simply be there. He was physically present, at least most of the time. That was supposed to be enough.

Dad worked in a manufacturing plant as a spot welder.

I remember him coming home from work at the end of the day, physically exhausted. He'd say hello to my mother, then wash up for dinner. Conversation around the table was pretty minimal, but it always included the question, "How was school today?" My sister and I would say, "Fine," and that was that. After dinner, Dad would retreat to the living room, plop down in "his" chair, and read the newspaper until he dozed off.

Sometimes we'd all gather around and listen to a program on the radio. This was in the days before television. But families could get glued to the radio just as they get glued to the TV today. Those were times of togetherness for our family, and I remember them warmly. I also remember that they didn't happen all that often.

Our house ran according to a fairly tight regimen. Dad was a strict disciplinarian who didn't like a lot of variance from the routine. As children we were expected to go about our business—chores, homework, even playtime—quietly and unobtrusively. And we usually did, having learned from unpleasant experience what happened when we awakened Dad's Irish temper.

Weekends likewise had a routine of their own. Dad spent most of Saturday working around the house, fixing things or just tinkering in the garage. He didn't involve us kids much in his tinkering.

Sunday was reserved for church. We went to church every week, morning and evening, without fail. On rare occasions, Sunday afternoons were special. We would go out to eat after morning service, then to the local art museum. It was in a lovely setting, with trees and a lake. When we were little, we got to run around the lake. As we got older, we spent more time inside the museum. I can still remember wandering through the musty old building, all by myself, entranced by the artifacts from Europe and Egypt and the Orient. I had a hunger to know more about what was going on beyond the horizons of my little world, about what had happened in the past. But most Sunday afternoons involved reading or taking a nap.

Dad did little to satisfy my hunger for knowledge. He didn't talk much, either about current events or, especially, about his own past. I knew he had grown up in Ireland, which sounded terribly exotic to me. But it was almost impossible to get him to talk about it. Sometimes we'd visit with Dad's brother, my uncle Tom. The women would congregate in the kitchen, and the men would gather in the living room, and the children were expected to stay out of the way. Sometimes I'd overhear bits and pieces of their conversations. I knew it wasn't my place to join in.

The fact was that we were all together as a family a lot of the time—at least physically. For all our togetherness, though, we maintained a definite emotional distance. Life in my family wasn't exactly like growing up on "Father Knows Best." But I think it was pretty typical for families in those days.

Mr. Mom?

What exactly was Dad supposed to do for us, anyway?

The traditional view of fathers and mothers was that Mom's work took place primarily within the home, while Dad's job was mostly outside the home—working to provide for the family's needs. Inside the home, he was little more than a supplemental mother, supporting Mom and backing her up when she was ill or otherwise absent from the scene.

Even today, to many people, "parenting" is pretty much synonymous with "mothering." According to this view, both parents need to build a bonded relationship with the children, provide nurturing care, allow the child to gradually move away from the parents so as to establish his or her individuality, etc. But this is simply to apply to both parents the job description for Mom.

That job description, in turn, derives from the view that the mother-child bond is essentially biologically determined. Mother and child begin the bonding process while the child is still in the womb. The unborn child hears her mother's voice, tastes her mother's food, even feels her mother's emotions. All this forms the basis for a close, symbiotic relationship after birth. The needs of the newborn and the mother are seen as complementary. Baby needs mothering, and Mom needs to mother. Everything fits together.

Mom seems to know what the baby wants or needs, without knowing how she knows it. She just knows whether the baby is hungry or sleepy or lonely—or just needs a new diaper. Dad may be mystified by this uncanny sixth sense. The baby's cries all sound pretty much the same to him. He marvels at his wife's ability to discern what is really going on.

Dad probably tries to be helpful in whatever ways he can. But in the early months, not many opportunities are open to him. Especially if Mom is nursing, Dad's ability to help out is pretty much limited to changing diapers or holding the baby for a few minutes while Mom attends to something else. Playing with the baby—especially the kind of roughhousing associated with the male role—is limited during the first few months. Most of what the baby needs can come only from the mother. Thus, at this stage, parenting really is more or less equivalent to mothering.

Unfortunately, too many fathers never seem to notice that infants turn into toddlers and schoolchildren and adolescents. They continue to think that caring for children is women's work.

My father engaged exclusively in "men's work"—meaning he went to work and brought home a paycheck. He also worked outside the house. He mowed the lawn, fixed the car, painted the house. Mom cooked the meals, washed the floors, and took care of the kids. The only time Mom and Dad broke out of their roles was when we kids broke out of our accepted behavioral patterns; then we faced Dad and his belt. Mothers were to be loved; fathers were to be respected—and feared.

Back then, many people saw the traditional roles of men and women as being almost sacred. Daughters were taught to cook, sew, clean the house, and look forward to marrying a man who would provide for them. Boys were expected to help with the heavy chores and look forward to getting a job that would provide for their families. A college education was seen as essential for sons, but only as an optional extra for daughters.

Sometime between when my father raised me and when I started raising my own children, things started to change.

Dr. Spock came along—soon followed by a host of other parenting experts whose books had an enormous impact on my generation. These experts argued vigorously for an expanded role for fathers. Dad was now urged to talk to the infant while it was still in the womb—trying, in some small measure, to compensate for the mother's innate advantage in prenatal bonding.

A generation later Dad, instead of pacing in the hospital waiting room during childbirth, would be invited into the delivery room itself, having learned how to coach his wife through labor and delivery (a role also once performed by women serving as midwives).

But while the father's role was expanded, it was still seen essentially as an extension of the mother's role. There was still no concept of a uniquely male role in childrearing. A conscientious father functioned as an assistant mother, though his major function was still to provide financial support and handle discipline—presumably from a more emotionally bonded position in the child's life.

In reality, most fathers faced a continuing conflict between work and home. Many found ways to be somewhat involved with their families and to father their children in positive, healthy ways. Many would have *liked* to do more with their families, but the demands of their jobs were too great—they left home early, came back late, and were too tired to do much more than collapse (in front of the television set, if they were fathers during the fifties or later). Some found more destructive ways to unwind, drinking themselves into relaxation or venting their pent-up anger on their wives and children.

I became a father in the midst of this transitional phase. I did far more with my children than my father ever did with me, and more than my friends' fathers ever did with them. But during the first years of my children's lives, I would have been hard-pressed to describe any unique role that I filled specifically as a *father*. Parenting was still just mothering, and in the end, mothering was what I did. I just did more of it than had been traditional for fathers in the past.

Desperately Seeking Daddy

Some researchers, like anthropologist Margaret Mead, suggest that fathering as we usually think of it is a purely human invention—that in fact fathers serve no function beyond what we see in animals. But if that is true—if fathers are so peripheral to healthy human development—then why do so many of us whose fathers were either physically absent or emotionally detached feel such an empty longing for Daddy?

If you have felt that longing, you are probably asking many of the same questions that family researchers have begun asking about fathers, fathering, and fatherhood.

The focus on fathers is a remarkably recent development. Until the last few years, Dad's role was not only downplayed, it was largely ignored by child development studies. Even today, with the new stirring of interest in the father's role, research remains scarce compared with the mountains of data and theoretical work devoted to the role of the mother. But enough research has been done and enough data assembled to allow me to say with confidence: *Our fathers, whether they were present or absent, have played a major role in shaping our lives.*

This is a fertile time for those who do research on the effects of absent fathers. Back in the 1940s, when I was growing up, most families were "together." I don't recall having a single childhood friend who came from a divorced home. As far as we were concerned, getting divorced was something that only the rich and irresponsible did. The very word *divorce* was seldom spoken out loud.

Things have certainly changed since then. It is now estimated that as many as one-third of today's children will experience their parents' divorce at some point in their lives. Of these, half will spend considerable time in a single-parent family. And the vast majority of these families will be headed by single mothers.[1]

In a study conducted at the University of Pennsylvania, researchers estimated that one out of four American children is being raised in a home without a father present. That works out to more than 15 million children growing up without a father. More than half these children, the researchers found, have never visited their father's new home. About 40 percent never even *see* their fathers during a typical year. These statistics cross racial, social, and even international boundaries. In France, almost two million children live in fatherless homes. In Canada the number is over 1.2 million.[2]

Dr. Louis Sullivan, Secretary of Health and Human Services in the Bush Administration, has noted that parents today spend 40 percent less time with their children than did parents in 1965. And that says nothing about the skyrocketing number of divorces: There are more than twice as many divorces now as there were just twenty-five years ago. According to Sullivan, the absence of fathers is "the greatest family challenge of our era."[3]

Only time will tell for sure what will happen to today's generation of fatherless or inadequately fathered children. But by studying the effects of father *absence,* we are beginning to learn more about the effects of father *presence.* More than ever before, we know how our own fathers' behavior affected the persons we have become. Behavioral scientists are learning what roles our fathers played in our development as children and adolescents. They are learning that Dad was not the same as Mom and that one parent, no matter how conscientious, was not the same as two.

The good news is that we are beginning to learn more about the significance of the father in the family. The bad news is that we are learning it by discovering how much damage has been wrought by absent, emotionally disconnected, or downright destructive fathers in the past.

There is no question that the absence of a father in the home brings serious consequences. For example, about half of all single-mother families live below the poverty line. The income of mothers who divorce typically drops by almost one-third. One result of this is that they are often forced to relocate frequently, subjecting the family to even greater stress and instability. The resulting lack of neighborhood support and relationship ties is often cited as one of the major negative effects of the absent-father family.[4]

What's more, the mother who is left to lead her family alone must try to fill the gap created by the father's absence. Her role becomes confused, and her frustration and fatigue increase, making her even less available to her children. She has no support, no backup, no sounding board for her parenting. Her child-rearing practices are often limited to meeting immediate needs and solving crises.

This is the picture for families where the father is *physically* absent. It doesn't take into consideration those homes where the father may be physically present, but so emotionally detached that he might as well not be there at all—or, worse, those families where the father's presence is itself a serious source of problems.

Some studies suggest that as many as 10 percent of fathers either physically or sexually abuse their children. It has been estimated that as many as one in five girls suffers from incest in the home. Perhaps it is not surprising, then, that in one survey troubled daughters said they went for comfort, first, to music; second, to girlfriends; and third, to television. Dad came in thirty-fourth.[5]

Counselors' offices today are filled with people searching desperately for Daddy—usually in all the wrong places. The fact that there is such a strong, innate hunger for a fatherly presence in our lives helps assure us that Dad is indeed essential to our development as healthy human beings. The fact that this hunger has gone unsatisfied in so many people, for so long, represents a serious deficiency for many of us.

There *is* healing for this wound. There *is* a way for us to satisfy our hunger for a father's presence in our lives. We'll talk about that in depth in later chapters. But before we can understand the solution and make it work in our own relationships, we need to come to grips with the problem.

As we walk through the pages of this book together, we'll take a close look at the forgotten father, at the way his role affects the lives of both sons and daughters. We will see the roles that only he can play in the family. And we will identify any destructive patterns we may have experienced, so we will know more clearly what constructive steps we must take if we are to experience healing.

TWO

What Only Dad Could Do

We were sitting in a rubber boat somewhere off the coast of Lahaina, Maui, in Hawaii. We were soaking wet. Not only was the water rough that day, but there was also heavy rain on and off. What on earth were we doing in this uncomfortable situation?

Looking at whales.

It was January, the time of year when humpback whales give birth to their babies, and we were hoping to catch a glimpse of one of nature's more extraordinary sights.

Suddenly we saw something a short distance off the starboard bow: a mother whale teaching her newborn baby how to breach. It was a remarkable sight. The mother would swim in close to the baby, put her nose down under the baby's midsection, and then toss the little one into the air. We got as close as we could as the fascinating ritual was repeated again and again.

Our guide told us to keep an eye out for other whales nearby. Earlier he had seen a mother and baby accompanied by two grown males. If this was the same group, there might be two more whales in the area. Sure enough, a few moments later someone on board our boat spied a large dorsal fin in the water a few hundred feet behind the mother and baby. Then we saw a waterspout go up about the same distance away, on the other side. It was an eerie feeling, floating around in a rubber boat, tossed by the waves and pelted by rain, knowing there were four whales cavorting in the vicinity!

Our guide pointed out that the males were deliberately keeping a respectful distance from the mother and her baby. They didn't want to upset the mother by interfering in the training of her offspring. They were not a part of the training process; among whales, apparently, teaching the young is considered women's work. The males were just waiting around for a chance to father the *next* baby.

As we noted in the first chapter, some people have argued that human fathers do not need to play any more of a part in the lives of their offspring than did those whales. Parenthood takes two, of course—a male and a female. But the male's task is limited to momentary participation in the act of procreation. The baby will be born nine months later (a bit longer than that for whales, by the way) whether the father hangs around or not. As for the rest of the parenting process, according to these people, fatherhood is simply a job description invented by society. As with the whales, the task of raising children is women's work; the men can just hang back in the distance, awaiting another opportunity to procreate.

Few researchers or theorists would put it quite that starkly, of course. But until recently, the almost universal lack of interest shown by developmental specialists in studying the role of the father certainly gives that impression. The focus of parenting studies has nearly always been on the mother. She is the one who is crucial to the child's development. Dad is an afterthought.

A change is in the air, however. We are starting to see a lot of data on the effects of fathers' *absence* in the lives of their children. A key feature of the burgeoning men's movement is discussion of absent fathers and the effect their absence has had in the lives of their sons. Such discussion is common among women as well. One British study found that more than one third of women in prison had been raised without fathers or had fathers who were notably weak and ineffectual.

Not long ago, I was participating in a radio call-in program about parents who were having problems with their children. Call after call came in, with one heartbreaking story after another of rebellious teenagers acting our their inner turmoil via involvement with drugs, sex, or other destructive behaviors. I asked each person who called, "Where's the father?"

In virtually every case the answer was, "Gone." One woman said her husband had departed the scene immediately after the birth of their youngest child.

"What about grandfathers or uncles?" I asked.

"All the men in our family are weak or absent," she replied.

In recent years, researchers have slowly begun to focus a bit more attention on *father* presence—the contribution of the father in child development, especially in relationship to their sons. In the observational work of Margaret Mahler in 1975,[1] Dad began to be acknowledged as having some specific tasks in relation to both sons and daughters. Researchers have now identified several important roles uniquely filled by fathers during different stages of their children's growth.

If you feel that your father has a lot to do with the person you are today, you are absolutely right. The rest of this chapter will help you understand what he did—or did not do—for you.

To understand the importance of Dad in a child's life, let's follow a pair of twins as they grow up. We'll call them Mike and Michelle.

Mike and Michelle are luckier than many; both their father and their mother are actively involved in their lives. Both parents were present when they were born, and both parents are still around to see them graduate from high school and begin their lives as young adults.

Early Childhood: Birth to Age Five

For the first three or four months of life, Mike and Michelle are in what is called the "autistic" stage of development. They are asleep more than they are awake, and even when they are awake they have little awareness of the outside world. (*Autism* means "detachment from the outside world." This is normal for newborns. It is a serious problem when it occurs in older children.)

Even though they are apparently detached, however, from the moment of their birth Mike and Michelle have been embarking on the accomplishment of their first major task in life: forging a *symbiotic* union with their mother. *(Symbiotic* roughly means "mutually necessary or beneficial.") There is an innate drive in the infant that causes him or her to seek to alleviate discomfort. This need is absolute in Mike and Michelle, and it is met by connecting emotionally with Mom.

The earliest manifestations of this drive are seen in the infant's "rooting" behavior, as it determinedly seeks out its mother's breast, as well as in other attaching behaviors. It is not hard to see why Mike and Michelle seek this kind of attachment. They have just left the safe, secure world of the womb, where every need they had was met before they even knew the need existed. Now, out in the cold, bright, stark world, they seek to recapture the security they felt in the womb—where they could hear Mom's voice, taste her food, even feel her emotions—by staying as intimately connected to Mom as possible.

Mom feels this need for attachment as well. Though the feeling is not absolute for her, as it is for the children—after all, without it they cannot survive—it is still quite powerful. The mother will actually regress in some ways in order to enter into the world of her babies. Her own schedule revolves almost entirely around theirs. She develops an uncanny ability to anticipate what they will need from her and when—the celebrated "sixth sense." She even starts speaking in baby talk, trying to connect interpersonally with these wonderful little creatures.

The early attachment phase, then, is important to Mom's physical and emotional health, and absolutely crucial to that of Mike and Michelle. But what about Dad?

At this stage, he is usually seen as important primarily as a backup to Mom (especially in our hypothetical example, since she is sure to be overwhelmed with twins!). In the past, most research focused almost entirely on this "second mother" role. But in recent years, researchers have started to point out the need for newborns to form bonded attachments to their fathers as well as to their mothers. Thus has grown the practice of inviting fathers into the birthing room to serve as the mother's "labor and delivery coach." Once Mom and baby leave the hospital, Dad will be encouraged to share some of the baby-care chores as well.

At first, Mike and Michelle will not really differentiate between Mom and Dad as individuals. They will relate to both of them essentially as "the mothering person" in their lives. But somewhere around the fourth month, researchers now believe, the children will begin to have some sense of Dad as distinct from Mom—though they will often continue to show a preference for Mom.

Somewhere between the ages of six and eight months, a second drive begins to assert itself in Mike's and Michelle's lives: the need to begin establishing themselves as separate individuals. They begin to crawl, and later to walk. These new behaviors both reflect and stake out an increasingly independent sphere of life. Mike's and Michelle's move toward greater independence is rooted in their confidence that the maternal bond is solid—thus it is safe to begin venturing out. A safe, trusting relationship with Mom is the foundation for growth toward autonomy.

As Mike and Michelle learn to get around by themselves, they become more adventurous, exploring their ever-expanding world. But not *too* adventurous. They are careful not to let Mom get too far away, or to stay out of sight for too long. If they go into a different room to play, they will periodically come back to make sure Mom is still there, or else they will call out to her from time to time, listening for her voice in response.

As Mike and Michelle approach their second year of life, they need to move further and further away from Mom in order to develop a sense of individuality. But in order to do this, they must have an emotional attachment with another person, so that the movement away from Mom can be attempted with some degree of emotional safety. Can you guess who this "other person" is?

Right—Dad. If the father is absent or severely uninvolved

with the child during this phase, the child may draw too close to Mom—the symbiotic fusion will continue too long and solidify too much. In other words, the child may become unable to differentiate himself or herself from Mom. Dependence on her may become so strong that the child's quest for autonomy is frustrated or smothered. If Dad is absent, Mom becomes too present and too powerful. Too much rests on the child's relationship with her. The child must be careful not to upset Mom, or she as well as Dad might be lost. Fear becomes the child's dominant emotion.

A typical crisis for children at this age has to do with how they handle their anger. Anger is a powerful emotion, and it is often frightening to children. They can easily feel that their anger may harm or destroy its object. At the same time, children seem to grasp instinctively that Mom and Dad are somehow connected to each other, which makes it safe to go to one of them when they are experiencing problems with the other one. In Mike's and Michelle's case, Dad is there. They have formed an attachment with him, and so they feel safe with their anger toward Mom.

This can be seen in little Michelle, who is frustrated and angry with Mom today. When she sees her father, she knows she can run to him and tell him about "mean Mommy." If she were left alone with these thoughts, her natural, naive sense of omnipotence might give her the impression that she could destroy her mother with anger. If Dad weren't there, Michelle would either keep pressing until her mother, in her own anger, put a stop to Michelle's acting-out behavior; or else she might repress her anger, turning it inward against herself, in order to "save Mommy."

Children raised in a home with only the mother present develop fear-based approaches to pleasing her. They feel that they had better not push Mom too far, lest they be utterly abandoned. Their behavior is often seen as ideal. In fact, it is often covering up conflicting emotions about Mom that are too terrifying for the child to think about.

But when little Michelle runs to Daddy and complains about how mean Mommy has been, she somehow knows that he will prevent any harm coming to Mommy as a result. Talking to Daddy makes it all okay. Michelle will be able to go back to Mommy later, her aggressive, angry feelings having been satisfied.

More and more, researchers are realizing that fathers do much more in the development of their preschool children than provide a buffer for Mom. Somewhere in the second half of the second year of life, the child begins to work through the foundations of his or her sexual identity. This process continues for many years, of course. But this particular, biologically determined period of time seems critical in terms of the child's understanding of what it means to be a boy or a girl, and it lays the foundation for the child's successful development into adult manhood or womanhood. Dad plays a central, unique part in this process of sexual identity formation.

By about eighteen months, Mike and Michelle can differentiate between pictures of boys and girls, men and women. Both of them are experiencing the need to move away from their mother, as I have described. But there is more going on as well. Mike is beginning to experience himself as *different* from his mother and to feel a closer bond to his father. In some special way, he starts to want to "be like Daddy."

Sexual identity begins to take shape in a variety of ways. For example, Dad plays differently with Mike than he does with Michelle. He roughhouses more with his son, and he is more gentle with his daughter. He is more sympathetic to Michelle's hurts and "boo-boos" than to Mike's cuts and scrapes. These seemingly minor things reinforce Mike's growing awareness that he and his father share some things in a unique way. Likewise, they reinforce Michelle's awareness that she and her father are different.

Significant father absence during early childhood has been linked to a number of problems occurring later in children's lives, including male homosexuality, adolescent drug abuse, delinquency, poor performance in school and on standardized tests, and childhood depression. More particularly, girls with missing fathers may grow to be women who are overly dependent on their mothers, have difficulty relating sexually, and are unable to work effectively.

Obviously, Dad does far more during the early-childhood years than merely provide an alternative, or even a complement, to Mom. The way he relates to his sons and daughters has a significant effect on the way they will grow to see themselves as men and women. At a more visceral level, Dad is important as a source of security and protection. When Mike brags that his father can beat up his friends' fathers, he is simply voicing his need for someone to keep him safe and secure. If Dad were absent, or manifestly weak and ineffective, Mike and Michelle would feel a sense of abandonment that could carry over into a host of adult insecurities.

I don't have any memories of my relationship with my father during this stage of my development. When I look at old photographs, I conclude that my father enjoyed his time with me. In the pictures, he looks like a proud father enjoying his son. He seems to be involved with me during family vacations. But I was born during the era when fathers were primarily providers. It was mothers' work to care for the children. So it is not surprising that I have no memories of him during my early childhood.

When I look back at my own experience as a father, I remember being quite comfortable with my children while they were infants and preschoolers. I enjoyed playing with them, roughhousing with them. I especially remember the minivacations we took to the beach in Florida. When we did things as a family, I was obviously needed to help take care of two little boys who were only thirteen months apart in age. My comfort level with my young sons indicates to me that I was able to give them what I had received from my father.

The same is true for me with my granddaughters. The times I spent with them before they started school were easy and enjoyable. Looking back, I realize that when the oldest started school several years ago, our relationship became more difficult. There were probably a number of reasons for this, but the main one is that I was comfortable giving what I had received, and uncomfortable being a father and a grandfather during the stages when my own father seemed uncomfortable with me.

The Father's Contribution During Early Childhood

1. Be a backup to Mom.
2. Be involved with the child so that she can form a bonded relationship with someone other than Mom.

3. Be available to the child so that he can move away from Mom and establish himself as a separate person.
4. Provide an outlet for the child's anger and frustration with Mom.
5. Lay the groundwork for development of the child's sexual identity.
6. Be a source of safety and security.
7. Lay a foundation for interaction in future years.
8. Provide a parenting model for the child.

The Elementary School Years: Ages Six to Twelve

Most research about child development stops at about age five. This is based on the belief that by this point most of the work is done—"the die is cast." And yet children who lose a parent after this age experience developmental problems that show the need for both parents at later stages and highlight the unique contribution each parent makes.

Understanding the major *life tasks* that Mike and Michelle are undertaking at this stage in their development helps us see where Dad makes his main contributions.

First, Mike and Michelle are learning to see themselves as productive individuals, able to take initiative in accomplishing goals. This involves harnessing their tremendous energy and channeling it into productive outlets. Fathers play a significant role in helping their children properly direct this energy, both by example and by influence. If Mike and Michelle succeed at this task, they will have laid the foundation for charting a life course later on. If they fail, they may feel a pervasive sense of guilt, or they may turn into perfectionists, always overcompensating for fear of failure.

Second, Mike and Michelle are beginning to develop competence in different skill areas, including language, other intellectual skills, and physical coordination. Success here will set the stage for long-term development of intellect—the way the mind perceives, assimilates, and organizes information—as well as other abilities, such as athletic skill and personal poise. Failure can lead to a sense of inadequacy and inferiority that carries over into the adult years.

Research shows that one clear consequence of losing a father between ages six and twelve is diminished academic achievement. Not only are standardized test scores lower for fatherless children, but teachers generally report a clear difference in both attitude and aptitude. Children from two-parent families, by and large, have higher grades and fewer behavioral and interpersonal problems than children from single-mother homes.

Third, Mike and Michelle are learning to contain and control their emotions and personalities. Fathers play an important part in helping their children learn to handle emotions, especially aggression. When the father is missing during this phase of life, the results are frequently obvious: The child's energy is dissipated, he or she lacks internal emotional discipline, and his or her unharnessed aggressiveness can lead to rebellious or delinquent behaviors.

Much of what Mike and Michelle are doing during this phase of their lives involves the development of cognitive (thinking) skill. Learning is easy and natural for them. Word pictures, numbers—all these symbols and the concepts they represent—seem fascinating, and Mike and Michelle grow rapidly in the ability to grasp, classify, and make use of them in a meaningful way.

Mike and Michelle are also majoring in social skills at this age. They are beginning to experience the complexity of human interaction, learning what it takes to get along with a with variety of people. Both parents play an important part in this, not only by providing a safe environment in which to learn and grow, but also by teaching, advising, modeling, and correcting as needed.

Mike and Michelle need both their parents during this time. Often they will have to move back and forth between them to get their needs met; when Mom is busy, Mike can go to Dad. When Dad comes home grumpy after a hard day at work, Mom can be there for Michelle.

Most of all, Mike and Michelle need both parents so that they can simply *be children*. When one parent is missing from the equation, there is a void in the family dynamic. In family life, as in physics, nature abhors a vacuum; children tend to try to "fill in" for the missing parent. Often they take on a level of responsibility that they are simply not equipped for. They face pressure to "grow up too fast." The process of human development is meant to take a number of years. When it is telescoped, or compressed, or hurried in this way, much of what is supposed to happen in that process gets short-circuited.

All too many adults look back at the years of their childhood and realize they were forced by circumstances to act like little adults in a child's body. They took on adult responsibilities without understanding why or how. In the end, childhood is skipped over and, as adults, there is a struggle with knowing how to play or enjoy life. Childlike fascination with the mysteries of life is foreign to them.

This is also the time for Mike and Michelle to clarify their respective sexual identities. Mike needs his father present to help him see what he himself is to become. By the same token, Michelle needs him present in order to see what she is not to become. This is a unique contribution from Dad. Mom cannot fill in the gap here if Dad is absent. Moreover, the way Michelle's father relates to her during this period of her life establishes many of the attitudes she will bear toward men for the rest of her life.

It's during my own grade school years that I am most aware of my father's emotional absence. I don't have any memory of his ever playing catch with me during this time or asking me to help him work on something in the garage or around the house. It wasn't that I didn't ask. It was more that he wasn't comfortable with me.

I remember one year when he painted the house during his vacation. I asked to help. He gave me a brush but, after a few strokes, took it back from me and told me I didn't know how to paint. Several weeks later I attended a Vacation Bible School at a nearby church. The craft project was to build and paint a birdhouse. I worked hard on my birdhouse because I wanted to finish it and paint it before the week was over.

I can still hear the teacher's words as he told me what a good painter I was. I couldn't wait to show my father. When I did, he was busy reading the paper. I remember him looking, nodding, and saying something like "That's nice" before turning back to his paper.

The teacher was impressed; my father wasn't.

I remember struggling to fit in with the other kids. I overcompensated at baseball and football so nobody would know how uncomfortable and insecure I felt. With a name like "Stoop," I was an endless source of fun for the other kids—and that didn't help my fitting in.

When my sons reached the elementary school years, I was determined to do things differently. But I felt awkward around Cub Scouts and Little League. When my third son started Little League, I finally took the risk of assisting as coach. During his last year I was the team manager. This was all new territory for me since my father had shown me very little about how to father during this stage of my children's development.

I felt insecure and threatened, but probably none of the other fathers noticed. Perhaps some of the same struggles were going on inside them.

The Father's Contribution During the Elementary School Years

1. Encourage the child to see herself as a productive individual.
2. Help the child develop competence in a variety of skill areas.
3. Foster healthy self-confidence in the child.
4. Help the child learn to contain and control his personality and emotions, especially anger.
5. Provide a safe environment for exploration and for learning both cognitive and social skills.
6. By active leadership in the family, free the child to be a child.
7. Clarify sexual identity for the child. Model what a son is to become and what a daughter is not to become.
8. Provide a parenting model for the child.

Adolescence: The Teen Years

The proper balance of power and responsibilities between Dad and Mom is especially important as children approach adolescence. Fathers make a particularly crucial contribution at the entry and exit points of this confusing, frustrating, and rewarding stage of life.

Adolescence is the gateway to adulthood. During the teen years, Mike and Michelle will vacillate between acting like children and acting like adults. This up-and-down behavior will increasingly frustrate their parents. But Mike and Michelle will successfully pass through the teen years and arrive at adulthood as healthy human beings. Dad will be a central figure in the process for both of them.

The beginning of adolescence is marked by what is called the Oedipal conflict. (This is different from what has sometimes been called the *Oedipal* stage of development, which is supposed to occur between the ages of three and seven.) The term comes from the ancient Greek story about Oedipus, the son of a king. When Oedipus is born, a seer foretells that when he grows up he will kill his father and marry his mother. In fear, his parents leave him to die. He is found and raised by others, however. As a young adult he returns to his home country, little dreaming that he has ever been there before. On the way, he gets into a fight with a man and kills him, not realizing that the man is his biological father. He later falls in love with the man's widow and marries her—neither of them realizing that she is his mother.

This story is often used to describe the near-universal experience of the emerging adolescent who, as his or her sexuality begins to emerge, falls in love with the parent of the opposite sex and competes with the same-sex parent in an effort to "win over" the object of his or her love. In its strong form, the incestuous overtones of this psychological model may seem repulsive. Yet it is generally accepted that all of us go through at least a mild form of this experience as we arrive on the doorstep of adolescence. As young boys enter puberty, they tend to draw closer to their mothers. There may not be any conscious sexual feelings involved. But there is often a desire to have Mom "all to themselves." Similarly, as girls enter puberty, they often become more attached to their fathers. Again, there is usually no overtly sexual content to this attachment, just a desire to be "Daddy's girl."

It's important for Mike and Michelle to feel this attachment to the opposite-sex parent. The parent will affirm them in their own developing manliness and womanliness and will show them how to relate to other people of the opposite sex. It's equally important for Mike and Michelle to have the same-sex parent present. This parent will teach them how to relate comfortably to two special people at the same time.

In earlier stages, the child typically relates to one parent at a time, often shifting the emphasis back and forth at various stages. Now he or she must learn to relate to both without losing either one. The technical term for this three-person relationship is *triad*. Mike and Michelle must learn to relate *triadically*.

This is not an easy task. It's too easy to make one person all-good and the other person all-bad, and this is indeed the way many of us attempt to relate to two others. Good emotional and social development, however, allow us to stay involved with both people at the same time. We are more likely to learn to relate triadically if Dad was present and involved in our lives when we were adolescents.

Mike and Michelle are fortunate that their father is a man of integrity and inner strength and that their parents' marriage is solid. One of the best forms of insurance for a safe passage through adolescence is the parents' marriage relationship. This is more than a good model of what marriage should be like. It is also an implicit message: Mom and Dad are indivisible. Problems often occur with adolescents who can come between Mom and Dad, getting the one to break ranks with the other. When this occurs, the triad breaks down. One parent is seen as all-good and supportive, and the other parent is seen as all-bad and not understanding. The adolescent is left with a false view of reality and the inability to relate to more than one person at a time.

Obviously the presence of the father, as a force equal to that of the mother, is essential if triangulation is to occur naturally. The father's absence or failure to participate can lead to all manner of difficulties for the developing child. Adolescents from mother-only families are more susceptible to destructive peer pressure than are other teens. They are statistically more likely to engage in sexual misbehavior. And daughters tend to repeat the pattern they have lived and to become single mothers themselves.

What exactly is Mike's father's role? A father needs to be an active presence for his son to compete with as the son tests out his newly emerging masculinity and sexuality. At some point, the father will need to lose this battle so that the son can become a man in his own right. But it is important that he not "cop out" on the struggle too soon. Mike's father actively engages his son, challenges him, and—when necessary—holds him in check. He is a strong and meaningful presence that Mike must deal with on his way to earning the right to feel like his father's equal.

At the same time, Michelle needs her father's presence in her life as she grows toward womanhood. Her developing sexuality is more obvious than Mike's, as her body changes noticeably from that of a girl into that of a woman. If a father is afraid to see his little girl grow up, the daughter will be fearful, too. She may feel that her father has rejected her, that she has somehow done something wrong, or that there is something shameful about being a woman. Many times, daughters who have felt rejected by their fathers during adolescence spend the rest of their lives searching unsuccessfully for father's love—usually looking in all the wrong places. Michelle's father is not only present; he admires and encourages his daughter, and she blossoms.

Adolescence is a time for Mike and Michelle to work through any earlier stages of development that are still incomplete. If they still feel any hurt from childhood experiences, this is the time to deal with it. If Dad recognizes any remaining problems from mistakes he made earlier, this is the time to correct them. For example, if Dad had been absent at earlier stages, and if Mom had compensated by being overwhelming or smothering, Dad could now help Mike and Michelle as adolescents work through these issues by serving as a strong counterbalancing presence to Mom.

My memory of my father during this stage of my life is that he was basically uninvolved. I couldn't get him and my mother to disagree on things regarding me, but I did figure out how to get around them, keeping them at a distance so I could do what I wanted. I avoided them by working—first at paper routes, then at the age of fifteen as a shoe salesman. Earning my own money gave me added independence. The hours away from home did the same thing. During my junior and senior years in high school, I worked full-time at the shoe store.

But the lack of involvement with my parents—especially my father—didn't help me grow up on the inside. I could work and make money like a man, but I stayed a boy emotionally. The struggles I experienced as a young adult, working with other adult men and yet feeling like a little boy inside, were directly related to the emotional distance I experienced within my family.

My father didn't know how to stay involved with me during that period of my life. His father had died just as he became a teenager. He had no model for being a father to an adolescent. As a result, I didn't have a model either. I really didn't know how to stay involved with my own adolescent sons.

One of our sons became heavily involved with drugs during adolescence. We all experienced a lot of pain and turmoil as a result. As he and I have talked about it as adults, he has pointed out that a major part of the problem back at the beginning stages was my lack of involvement in his life. I had thought I was available to my kids, even though I was busy with my own career and with finishing my schooling. But as my son and I talked, I realized I was not emotionally available to them at that time.

I didn't really know how to be.

The father is also essential for something that is often over-looked in our culture, something that has to do with the successful conclusion of adolescence. In Bible times, it was called "the blessing." Modern people are often mystified by the Bible story of the patriarch Isaac and his sons, Esau and Jacob. Rebekah, their mother, goes to great lengths to manipulate the situation and trick Isaac into giving his blessing to Jacob instead of to Esau, the firstborn. This paternal blessing, which may seem trivial and incidental to us, was seen in Bible times as an essential step in a boy's passage into manhood.

In reality, a paternal blessing is still essential for both sons and daughters.

Adolescence must come to an end. We all know men and women who seem to be trying to remain eternal adolescents. They simply have never grown up. They go through life acting like irresponsible, fun-loving, thrill-seeking kids. Invariably, these are people who have never experienced a definite closure to adolescence. Both Mike and Michelle need some form of the father's blessing to mark the end of childhood and the arrival of adulthood.

Many of us are still looking for that father's blessing. Not surprisingly, we are looking for it in the logical place: our fathers. One man told me that all he wanted in life was for his father to put his arm around him and say, "Son, you're doing great."

Sadly, his father died before he was able to talk to him about what he needed and wanted. The man felt lost, as if he were somehow unable to graduate from the awkwardness of adolescence into confident manhood. He was excited to learn that even though his father was gone, it was still possible to make peace with him and to complete this important piece of unfinished business.

The Father's Contribution During Adolescence

1. Teach the child how to relate triadically (to two other people at the same time).
2. Be a source of competition and modeling for a son as he grows toward manhood.
3. Affirm a daughter's femininity and her growth toward womanhood.
4. Be available to resolve any leftover issues from the earlier stages of development.
5. Make his inner strength and stability available to the child, providing a counterbalance to the roller coaster of adolescence.
6. Model a good marriage relationship.
7. Present a unified authority with the mother to prevent the child from "splitting."
8. Provide a blessing as the child moves into adulthood.
9. Provide a parenting model for the child.

In this chapter we have seen how our father's active involvement was crucial at every stage of our development. Though it was subtle, his loving presence and concerned involvement were paramount in forging our self-esteem. Sometimes Dad merely supplemented what Mom was doing. But most of the time he made a vital contribution all his own. In fact, as we'll see in the next chapter, he had four basic roles in our life— each of which came prominently into play at different stages of our development.

THREE

The Four Roles of Fathers

What type of father did you have?

It's a difficult question to answer. All fathers are different. We all recognize that. There is no single style of fathering that can be prescribed for everyone. In fact, there are as many different *types* of fathers as there are *fathers*. Each one inevitably brings his own unique set of gifts, qualities, strengths, and weaknesses to the job.

But as we look out over the whole realm of what it means to be a father, certain patterns begin to emerge. We find that we can usefully speak of four general types of fathers, or rather, four different roles that fathers can play in the lives of their children. As we'll see, each of the roles is important, and each should be part of every father's approach to his children.

Below you will find the Fathering Roles Inventory, a simple exercise to help clarify the four roles of fathers. Take out a pencil and do it now, before you read further. Not only will it help you learn what the roles are; it will also help you understand where your father was strong—and where he was weak.

Fathering Roles Inventory

Below are seven statements, each of which may be completed in one of four ways.

In the column on the left, check the option that represents

the value that is most important to you.

Check the column on the right that reflects your perception of your father's probable values.

1. When making a decision, the most important thing is to

My opinion   **How I think my father would answer**

_____ a. quickly size up the task and "just do it."   _____
_____ b. consider the big picture and take every-   _____
            thing into account.
_____ c. make a pro-and-con list and follow it.   _____
_____ d. learn how to listen to your heart.   _____

2. Before beginning a task, it is most important to

My opinion   **How I think my father would answer**

_____ a. identify the most efficient way to do   _____
            the task
_____ b. consider all the possible ways of going   _____
            about the task
_____ c. get the facts in order.   _____
_____ d. identify the values that are at stake.   _____

3. The most important thing a father can do for his children is to

My opinion   **How I think my father would answer**

_____ a. stand by them; even fight for them if   _____
            necessary.
_____ b. help them see the bigger picture.   _____
_____ c. teach them how to think for themselves._____
_____ d. genuinely show care and love for them. _____

4. One of the things I admire most in a father is that he

My opinion   **How I think my father would answer**

_____ a. is actively involved with his children.   _____

_____ b. encourages his children to accomplish   _____
their dreams.
_____ c. is clear about what he expects from his   _____
children.
_____ d. shows love to his children no matter   _____
what.

5. In solving problems, one should first

My opinion   **How I think my father would answer**

_____ a. just jump in and deal with the prob-   _____
lem.
_____ b. take the time to consider all the poss-   _____
ible solutions.
_____ c. simply consider what is the right solu-   _____
tion.
_____ d. consider how any solution will affect   _____
the other people involved.

6. In a conflict, one should focus on

My opinion   **How I think my father would answer**

_____ a. doing something quickly to resolve the   _____
problem.
_____ b. letting time resolve the conflict.   _____
_____ c. who is right and who is wrong.   _____
_____ d. how to keep the peace.   _____

7. When facing an extremely difficult situation, are you most

likely to ask

My opinion   **How I think my father would answer**

_____ a. will things get worse if we don't act now?

_____
_____ b. is there a better way to deal with this   _____
situation?
_____ c. what is really fair here?   _____
_____ d. whose feelings are getting hurt in this   _____
situation?

My opinion	**How I think my father would answer**

Total answers for "a" _____ _____

These characteristics represent the *warrior/protector* role.

Total answers for "b" _____ _____

These characteristics represent the *spiritual mentor* role.

Total answers for "c" _____ _____

These characteristics represent the *lawgiver* role.

Total answers for "d" _____ _____

These characteristics represent the *loving nurturer* role.

Did you find it difficult to choose among the options? Did they all seem important to you? Well, they *are* all important. Was there one role that had more responses than any others? The four options help identify four characteristic roles that fathers play in their children's lives. The "a" responses identify the role of a *warrior/protector;* the "b" responses identify the role of a *spiritual mentor;* the "c" responses identify the role of a *lawgiver;* and the "d" responses identify the role of a *loving nurturer.* The letter with the highest number of responses identifies the role that you value the most. The right column identifies the role that your father probably found came more naturally to him. Usually, one of the roles will be dominant in a father's parenting style.

Different roles are typically more crucial at different stages of the child's development. Ideally, every father should be able to play all four roles, and be able to emphasize the one that is most needed in the life of each individual child at that point.

Let's look now at the characteristics of each role.

The Nurturer

This role is of primary importance to the child between birth and age five.

When Jeremy took the Fathering Roles Inventory, he had no trouble identifying the responses that were characteristic of his father. He described his father as a classic nurturer, a man who was free with his emotions and able to express love and affection without hesitancy. He lived life with a passion.

In some ways, the roles played by Jeremy's parents were reversed from those of the typical family. He saw his mother as strong, even tough; a rigid disciplinarian who had difficulty expressing her feelings. "Dad was clearly the center of warmth in our family," Jeremy recalled. (Incidentally, though it occurred in Jeremy's family, a nurturing father will not necessarily have a non-nurturing wife.)

As we talked, Jeremy filled in some images of what his father was like. "We always knew he cared," Jeremy said. "He was very empathetic. Any time we were struggling with something, we always knew that he was the one to talk to. I guess most kids would run to their mother at times like that, but not us."

Jeremy's father was a frustrated artist who had to work in an automotive repair shop all his life. Jeremy was certain that, had the circumstances of his life been different, his father would have excelled at something artistic. Family outings frequently featured visits to art galleries or other museums. When they traveled, his father always knew if there was an interesting museum in the area, and they would usually stop there.

Jeremy remembers his father as very tender and sensitive. He recalls times when he saw his father fight back tears after his wife had said something harsh or cold. He was "touchy" in other ways, too—always throwing his arms around the kids, giving them hugs. Jeremy remembers being embarrassed that his father insisted on kissing him. "I thought I was too old for that," he laughs. "But now, looking back, I can see that it was just his way of being affectionate. He never did anything inappropriate or wrong. He was just more demonstrative than most fathers."

The oldest of four children, Jeremy was thirteen when the last child was born, and he clearly remembers his father's enjoyment of his new daughter. "More often than not, it was Dad who got up with her at night," Jeremy remembers. "He was almost more of a mother to her than Mom was. Not that Mom wasn't a good mother—Dad just really enjoyed it, and he did it really well. Actually, they seemed like a pretty good team."

Obviously, the nurturer role was dominant in Jeremy's father. Right up to the day he died, Jeremy's father was fully alive and free to express his feelings: "It was like he had an inner joy that just radiated out of him when he was with his kids," Jeremy remembers.

This is typical of nurturers. They have a deep-rooted "centeredness" within themselves that imparts strength to those around them. Their children feel secure—*valued*—because by being receptive to their children's emotions, nurturers validate a core part of their children's identities. At the same time, they model for their children the ability to take another person's perspective. This ability doesn't come automatically—it is something children need to learn by example.

Sometimes we see a father whose natural dominant role might be that of a nurturer but who, because of his own problems, has shut down that part of himself. He may drown his feelings in alcohol, or run from them by working all the time, or retreat into silence and isolation because the emotions aroused by being with his family are too intense and make him afraid. Such a father often becomes a harsh disciplinarian. He is afraid of his own feelings, so he lashes out at those close to him in an effort to keep their emotions at arm's length.

My own father fit this description. He was a very emotional man, but he carefully kept his emotions to himself. He seemed to love his family a lot, but he didn't really know how to communicate those feelings. Now that I understand his experiences as a child, including the loss of his father, I think I know what happened: He had shut himself down emotionally long before he became a father, and when he had his own family, he didn't know how to open himself up again. So his emotional and nurturing side stayed locked inside. What I remember experiencing instead was his harshness and his bad temper.

The Bible offers a portrait of a nurturing father (one whose nurturing role gets out of balance with the other roles) in the person of King David. David's warm, tender side come through clearly in the Psalms, and it is also reflected in the loyalty and integrity he often displayed in relationships with others. Unfortunately, the fact that his dominant nurturer role was not balanced with the other roles led him into great difficulty and pain.

A father who does not go beyond the nurturing role is often incapable of setting clear limits for his children. When they do wrong, he is eager to understand. He is usually unwilling to confront them when they transgress his limits. We see this trait in David when one of his sons, Amnon, rapes his half sister Tamar. Absalom, another of David's sons and Tamar's full brother, is furious. Although David empathizes with Absalom's anger and with Tamar's shame, he seems paralyzed, unable to take decisive corrective action.

Enraged by his father's lack of response, Absalom decides to take matters into his own hands and kill Amnon. David learns of Absalom's vengeful deed and is overwhelmed with grief. Still he does nothing.

Absalom flees from Jerusalem and is gone for more than three years. Even though Absalom is his favorite, David does nothing to contact him or bring him back. David's friend Joab arranges for a wise woman from Tekoa to confront David about his unjust behavior toward his son. David finally instructs Joab to bring Absalom home and then, in one of the saddest episodes in his life, David still cannot bring himself to face his son for another two years.

Here is an extreme example of a nurturing father who is not making use of the other sides of fathering. As a result, in the end even his nurturing is blocked. How different the rest of Absalom's life might have been had his father sought him out and restored their relationship! Instead, Absalom's anger at his father's silence festered until he finally led a revolt against David—and ended up being killed by Joab.

It is normal that one particular role will be dominant in every father's approach to parenting. It will become his strength, his "style." I remember nurturing as a strength of my own father. He was apparently able to show more nurturing when I was little than when I grew older. It was as if when I was a preschooler, I was not a threat to him. He could relate to me then.

He was more nurturing with my sister than with me, maintaining his warm relationship with her beyond her early childhood years. Perhaps he could relate more easily to a daughter than to a son. Or perhaps he, like many fathers, connected more with the second child than with the first, since a mother can't be as exclusively occupied with the second child as she was when she had only one child.

As I grew older, I needed to draw on other aspects of my father. I needed a lawgiver, a warrior/protector, a spiritual mentor. In these areas, however, my father dropped the ball. He did not know how to relate to his growing son because he had developed only one side of himself.

My own strength as a father is also as a nurturer, especially to very young children. I felt quite comfortable being nurturing to my sons during their preschool years. I am still struck by little children—particularly my grandchildren. But I notice that as they begin school I grow less comfortable in my relationship with them. It seems to take more time and effort on my part. I am indeed my father's son.

To be a balanced father, however, a man must be able to access and utilize the other roles, as well as his primary role. The weakness of the nurturing father will invariably be an inability to set firm limits for his children and to follow through in enforcing them. Typically, the nurturing father needs to work especially hard at developing the "lawgiving" role.

In Jeremy's family, the mother set and enforced the limits. Often when the father is tender and warm, the mother will gravitate to the disciplinarian's role. But this is not meant to be the mother's primary role. As we'll see in the next section, the father should be the main lawgiver. Even so, had Jeremy's mother not stepped in as she did, Jeremy might have experienced something akin to what Absalom experienced. She provided the structure to life, without which Jeremy might have experienced his father as "wishy-washy"—the way Absalom saw David.

Children need nurturing all their lives, but especially during the first five years. When they experience Dad as warm and caring, they are able to bond with him, as well as with Mom, in a way that makes them feel safe and secure. As we will see in the next chapter, this becomes especially important when the time comes for the child to begin drawing away from the mother.

The Lawgiver

This role is of primary importance to the child between the ages of six and twelve.

There was never any question in Megan's house as to who was in charge. "I don't mean that Dad was mean, and he was certainly never abusive," Megan said. "I just mean that we always knew he was the boss. His word was law." Fathers whose dominant role is that of the authoritative lawgiver are usually seen as "firmly in the saddle" of family life. Some of them can be controlling or abusive. That, in fact, is the common stereotype. It is important to understand, however, that this role definitely can—and should—be expressed in healthy and life-giving ways.

"We always knew where we stood with Dad," Megan said. "It

was like that television commercial: 'The best surprise is no surprise.' The rules were clear, and they were enforced fairly. Sometimes I look back on my childhood, and I wish Daddy and I could have been closer. But I'd never trade the security and self-respect he gave me."

One of the things a father needs to model for his family is the ability to approach life with competence and confidence. How does he handle problems that confront the family? Can he deal with each of the children fairly and respectfully? Does he act with integrity and high moral standards? Both sons and daughters want to know that their father is there for them, that he is someone who can be counted on, like a rock. These are qualities that children are especially attuned to during the elementary school years.

In Megan's family, Mom and Dad fit the traditional pattern: Mom was the warm, caring figure, and Dad was the authority. "I always felt that everyone's opinions and desires were respected," Megan recalls. "But when the time came to make a decision, we looked to Dad. And he always acted as though that was the way it was supposed to be."

The theme that came up over and over again as Megan talked about her father was his quiet strength. She never saw him as overpowering, only as solid and strong. This is not always an easy balance to find: The lawgiver can easily cross the line and become a tyrant. Or, on the other side, he can retreat into silent detachment.

When I think of an example of a lawgiving father who is out of balance, I think of the title character in Pat Conroy's novel *The Great Santini.* Marine Lieutenant Colonel "Bull" Meacham treats his children as though they are new recruits and he is their drill sergeant. When the family moves to a new location, Bull lines the boys up on the front steps and gives them a forceful lecture on how they will and will not conduct themselves in their new environment. Unfortunately, he is totally insensitive to what his boys are experiencing as a result of the move.

Bull Meacham believed in his authority, but the lawgiver role seems to be the only one he was conversant with. Bull acted authoritarian in the belief that it would make his sons strong. Instead, he undermined their confidence and made them fear him and life. Harsh, authoritarian fathers often produce passive, fearful children.

Brian's father must have been a lot like Bull Meacham. A career army man, he had risen to the highest rank open to an enlisted man: staff sergeant. As a child, Brian idolized his father. But when he reached adolescence, he and his father began to collide head-on. Brian left home before he even finished high school. His father was devastated, but he never let anyone know how he felt.

Brian got into drugs. On several occasions he spent time in jail. No matter what happened, though, he refused to call his parents for help. "I'd rather fight it out my own way than face my father's anger for not doing it his way," Brian said. "I called my mother's parents a couple times, and they promised not to tell my folks anything. I'm sure they did anyway. But I was glad just to have someone to call during that time."

Brian came to our clinic to deal with his addictions. "I always knew right from wrong," he told his aftercare support group. "You couldn't live six months with my dad without knowing that much. But that was all you'd get from him. I never felt like he loved me or even understood me. I figured he didn't care, so why should I? Now I can see that he was just lopsided. He only knew how to be one certain way. Kids need more than that from their parents."

Remember what we said earlier: Although fathers who are lawgivers fulfill an important role in their children's lives, the lawgiver role needs to be balanced with the other roles. Lawgivers seem to have the hardest time integrating the nurturing role into their approach. Without that counterbalance, however, their children will often grow up fearful, incapable of making good decisions on their own.

The prophet Nathan offers a biblical example of a good balance between lawgiver and nurturer (see 2 Samuel 12). Nathan has a longstanding relationship with King David. He is not David's father, of course, but he still serves as a model of how the lawgiving role can work when it is balanced by other roles, especially by the nurturer role.

God reveals to Nathan the details of David's adultery with Bathsheba and the subsequent arranged death of her husband. Rather than simply confront David with his knowledge, Nathan tells the king a story to capture his attention. As he talks, he probably studies the king's face carefully, watching for signs that David has got the point. Then, at the moment when David expresses outrage at the injustice perpetrated by the man in Nathan's story, Nathan gives him the punch line: "Thou art the man!"

David's own sense of right and wrong is able to break through the shell of denial and self-deception he has built around himself. In deep sorrow and brokenness, he seeks forgiveness for his sins.

Nathan "laid down the law," all right. But because he combined lawgiving with obvious concern for David and an appeal to his tender, caring side, he was able to be far more effective than he would have been had he simply insisted that the king do the right thing.

Lawgiving is a role unique to fathers. This does not mean that mothers do not train children to distinguish right from wrong or that they do not provide any family discipline. Lawgiving, however, is more than setting and enforcing rules and standards. The father's lawgiving role has a symbolic influence that is greater than his specific actions. If I know Dad is there and that he is involved in my life, I will have an inner sense of security and structure that goes beyond the concept of laws or of knowing right from wrong.

Perhaps the British understand this with their monarchy. Most of the function of the king or queen of England is symbolic. Yet to an English person, England without the king or queen is unthinkable—it isn't England anymore. In the same way, the father fulfills a role during this period of a child's life that defines the family. It goes deeper than merely setting the standards. It is at the core of what is involved in growing into adulthood. Father is there as the lawgiver.

When lawgiving is balanced with nurturing, a father helps his children learn to make decisions about right and wrong for themselves. It is not just a matter of "following orders." When it comes to rules and standards of behavior, children operate on a "show me, don't tell me" basis. They need to see morality modeled, struggled with, confronted, and dealt with realistically and honestly. A father who is comfortably balanced in his lawgiving role is able to *demonstrate* his sense of integrity and morality by the way he relates to his children, not just *proclaim* it to them.

With sons, for example, even in horseplay there can be a sense of respect for the son as a person—such as by listening and responding appropriately when the son says, "That's enough." When his son is feeling embarrassed or humiliated, the father can make it a point to take his discomfort seriously, to help him work through the emotions and issues involved, rather than simply say, "Snap out of it." Now, there may well come a time when "Snap out of it" is precisely the right thing to say—but that time will be seen more clearly in the context of a supportive, nurturing attitude. When Dad allows himself to relate openly and honestly with his son, it's catching.

A daughter, likewise, needs to experience her father's loving appreciation of her abilities. Many fathers don't quite know what to make of little girls. The things their daughters are interested in tend to be alien to them; the things fathers are interested in often have little relevance to their daughters. Nevertheless, when they notice and express appreciation for a daughter's interests and accomplishments, they help set the stage for effective exercise of the lawgiver role. Lawgiving is only effective when done in the context of love and nurture. Nothing helps a daughter develop confidence in her femininity more than the knowledge that she is "Daddy's special girl."

At this stage of life, both sons and daughters tend to idealize Dad. He is their hero. He can do no wrong. If he is absent, or if he *does* do wrong, their tendency will be to deny the weakness and failure they see. They may instead focus on themselves as the source of the problems they are experiencing. Children who do this often grow up to have great difficulties in adult relationships, especially in marriage.

My father tried to be a lawgiver, but he ended up simply being harsh. Unable to be open with his emotions, he had difficulty with this important role. Since he was a harsh disciplinarian, the first thing I learned from him was to avoid him and his temper. The second thing was not to trust authority. Adolescent experiences with several police officers added to my distrust, but my relationship with my father was at the root of my personal struggle with authority figures.

The lawgiver role is especially important during the elementary school years. Studies have shown that when the father is not involved with his children, or when he is too harsh—in other words, when the children miss out on the lawgiving function during this stage—they often grow up to have significant problems relating to all authority figures.

The Warrior/Protector

This role is of primary importance to the child between the ages of twelve and eighteen.

I chose the word *warrior* for this role because the stage of adolescence so often seems like a battle, for both parents and children. Adolescence begins, not when the child turns thirteen, but when he or she enters puberty. The physical changes that occur in puberty are accompanied by hormonal changes, emotional changes, and attitudinal changes. Social and cultural factors are also thrown into the mix as the child enters the teenage world.

At this stage, Dad needs to know how to fight for his children in two senses. First, he needs to stand *with* them, fighting on their side as it were, confronting the confusing and frustrating changes that threaten to overwhelm both him and them. Second, he needs to fight *against* the forces that try to draw his children away from or even place them in opposition to himself. Some of these forces come from the surrounding culture. Some arise from within the adolescent. Others arise from within the father.

In order to fight for his children, the father must stay involved with them. Can he let his relationship with his daughter evolve as she changes from a little girl into a young woman? Can he give his son room to become a man? These are crucial questions for the warrior to grapple with.

At the heart of the warrior role is the father's ability to be aggressive. The warrior father will channel his aggressiveness with his children so that he can actively engage and challenge them, but without always needing to win. He can take pleasure when his children master new skills—even when they surpass him.

Wendy was thirty-eight, the oldest of three girls, and had never married. When I asked her to tell me about her father, she said, "We love to play tennis. Our whole family does. Well, everyone but Mom. She says she hates tennis. Dad is pretty good at it, but I'm better. I'm the only one in the family who can beat him on a regular basis."

Then she added, "It makes him mad when I beat him. But I sort of enjoy it."

Wendy's father was clearly competitive by nature. That in itself was not a problem. The problem was his inability to lose gracefully. His need to defeat his children, even at tennis, made it hard for them to grow up. The only way for them to become adults was to beat him at his own game—and even then, victory was bitter. In her father's world, there was room at the top for only one person—and Wendy's father wasn't about to "get off the court."

The warrior's goal must not be to win, but to help his children sharpen their skills. If he overpowers them, they will become discouraged. If he yields too easily, on the other hand, they will not develop the inner strength to draw on when he is not around.

We often think of the warrior role of the male in relation to his work. We say, "It's a jungle out there," or "You've got to fight to get ahead in this world," or, as someone once put it, "Capitalism is war with the gloves off." Rick Fields points out that the "emphasis on competition led many American businesspeople and management consultants to think of business as war. This view was strengthened by the use of military language to describe business conflicts. There were trade wars, advertising campaigns, market blitzes, corporate raids, and sales forces.... There were even headhunters who specialized in recruiting executives."[1]

Part of the father's task in this role is to prepare his child to battle effectively with life, whether in business or at home. Some fathers fail in the warrior role because all their aggressiveness is channeled into their work, leaving little time or energy for involvement with their children. Others fail because they cannot contain their aggressiveness; they continue to challenge their children long after the battle is supposed to be over. Still others become abusive, trying to force their children into a state of permanent dependency.

The battle begins with the Oedipal conflict. Many anthropologists believe that the formal initiatory rites into manhood in some of the more primitive cultures are a direct result of the universality of this conflict at the beginning of adolescent development. Let's take a look at how this conflict works, first for daughters, and then for sons.

As a girl enters puberty, she begins to discover her sexual feelings and to become interested in males. Her father, as the primary male in her life, becomes a focus of this newly emerging interest. This does not mean that she desires a sexual relationship with him (though some fathers actually believe this to be the case and use it as an excuse for imposing an incestuous relationship). At this stage, she is not capable of sexualizing her feelings. She simply feels attracted to her father in a way she has not felt before.

She may act on these new feelings in a variety of ways. She may feel frightened by them and pull back from her father. Or she may "flirt" with him, just to see what flirting is like with her favorite male. Either way, what she is trying to find out from this extraordinarily important person in her life is this: *Do you approve of what's happening to me?*

As a warrior, the father's response is to act as his daughter's protector in ways that affirm her emerging femininity. He must fight against any tendency to back away from her, fight to stay involved with her, showing her respectful attention and admiration.

He also needs to be affirming amidst the emotional struggles that accompany her hormonal changes. If the father is uncomfortable with his own emotions, he may simply turn his daughter away: "Go talk to your mother." This will be his daughter's loss.

One woman said about her warrior father, "The most generous thing he ever did for me was to tell me he loved me." An adolescent—male or female—who gets that message from Dad is far better equipped to cope with the struggles of adolescence.

Wendy's father had been uncomfortable with her emergence into womanhood. As her body changed, he refused to acknowledge it. He continued to treat her as a tomboy, competing with her not only in tennis but in everything else they did.

"He stopped touching me," Wendy recalls. "I think he was embarrassed by what was happening and just didn't know what to do or say about it. I kept competing with him because it was the only way to stay involved with him." Years later Wendy was still struggling to accept herself as a woman, to feel feminine—especially around other men.

Every warrior needs to know when to fight and when to retreat. In Wendy's case, her father retreated at precisely the point when he most needed to stay involved. And in the end, they both lost. Wendy saw her father as weak because he didn't have the courage to face what was happening. "He did the same thing with both my sisters," Wendy said. "They're both married, but both their husbands are wimps. I wouldn't want to be married to someone like that."

Warriors are "doers" and they tend to feel that they are doing their job as long as they are doing *something*. Wendy's father felt he was being a good father because he was always playing tennis or some other sport with his daughters. He was very uncomfortable with the idea of just being with them, doing nothing in particular.

"I suppose he was afraid we'd ask him something he didn't know about or didn't know how to deal with," Wendy said. "I think he was afraid to let us really get to know him."

The warrior father needs to stay involved with his daughter and, at the same time, nurture his relationship with his wife. If the connection between father and mother is solid during this stage, the daughter is free to pursue a new kind of relationship with Dad without the internal conflict of feeling that she is somehow undermining Mom. She is able to feel good about herself as a woman and about her ability to relate successfully to men.

Sons face a different kind of battle. According to the Oedipal model, the son fights with the father for the attention of the mother. If he wins—either because the father has not developed in his warrior role or because the father is absent— he will forever be a "mama's boy." And all too many sons do win, either because their fathers never show up for the battle or because they so adamantly refuse to give any ground at all that the son remains a child until his father dies.

At the beginning of puberty, boys begin to notice the females of the species. At first these stirrings are strange and alarming, so the boy is drawn toward the one woman he knows is safe—his mother. As with the attraction between daughter and father, this interest is not overtly sexual, even though it does occur as the result of awakening sexuality. Even so, the son may relate to his father as a rival for Mom's attention. As he asserts his masculinity, the father needs to stay involved with him—to compete with him, so to speak, for the lead male position in the family.

Bob's father did precisely that. As he looks back on that phase of his life, Bob remembers his father spending more time with him, taking a more detailed interest in his life. They had started doing various things together some years before, so that when Bob reached age thirteen, he and his father already had some well-established common interests.

One of the things they especially enjoyed was playing golf together. When Bob was only seven, his father had given him a set of sawed-off golf clubs. At that age, golf was just a fun way to spend time with Dad. But as he grew older and his physical coordination matured, he began to challenge his father's supremacy on the course. There was a lot of good-natured kidding as Bob's scores caught up with and then surpassed his father's.

Unlike Wendy's father, who couldn't stand to lose at tennis, Bob's father enjoyed his son's increasing prowess. Competition was secondary to the enjoyment that came from being together. The healthy quality of their rivalry on the golf course carried over into other areas as well.

"I always knew Dad was on my side," Bob said. "He never resented it when I got better than him at something. It was as though he took satisfaction that something he loved would live on through me."

Most important, even as he overtook his father in other areas, Bob knew he couldn't beat his father in relating to

Mom. Dad was always number one there. Because Bob could see a solid relationship between his parents, he was able to contain his new sexual awareness and direct it in ways appropriate to his age.

It is a difficult balance that a father needs to maintain with his son during this stage of development. On the one hand, he needs to provide a strong foil for his son to work against. He can't just back down and let his son win; that would only model weakness and devalue the victory. On the other hand, he cannot be overpowering, or he will stunt the very growth in personality he is trying to foster. It is in this sense that the father is warrior and protector, both at the same time.

As messed up as his life was in many respects, King Saul appears to have been a reasonably good father, at least in fulfilling this particular role. He was, to say the least, a disappointment as a king, and he was erratic and unpredictable as a military man—sometimes he led with brilliance, at other times he was paralyzed by fear. In his relationship with his sons, however, Saul appears to have been a solid, well-balanced warrior/protector father. We see in Saul's history none of the terrible problems that plagued David and his sons.

I have always been fascinated by Saul's apparent gifts as a father, especially in terms of his son Jonathan. Jonathan had all the markings of a great future king. He had great courage, being willing to take on a whole camp full of Philistines practically single-handedly. He was sensitive and loyal; like his brothers, he was to die in combat at his father's side. Yet Saul seems never to have been jealous of Jonathan's gifts—he reserved his jealousy for David.

In a nutshell, what the warrior father does at this stage of his children's lives is to encourage the unfolding of the aggressive drive that will make the difference between their success and failure as adults. By harnessing his aggressiveness in relation to his children, this father helps his children successfully harness and direct their own aggressiveness. When a father fails in this role—either by being too aggressive and domineering, or by withdrawing and being too passive—it is invariably reflected in work difficulties in his adult children.

As a young man, I often struggled with authority issues in my work. I solved those problems by changing positions a lot. It wasn't that I got into trouble with the boss—I was too passive for that. It was more that I grew dissatisfied with my position and resolved that issue by finding another job.

For years, my length of stay at any place I worked was about two-and-a-half years. I used to say that it took me six months to figure out what I needed to do, a year to get bored doing it, and then six months to find a new position. As I look back, I realize that I was avoiding issues of authority. In many ways, this was a consequence of the lack of relationship with my father during my adolescent years.

I was always a hard worker—I saw that modeled in my father. But because he was a distant authority figure to me, I was uncomfortable getting too close to authority figures at work. When I finally made peace with my father, I found that I also made peace with other authority figures in my life. I wish I had done it earlier, for that would have helped me to be more available to my own children during their adolescence.

The apostle Paul helps us reflect on the warrior/protector role when he warns fathers in one place not to exasperate their children (by being too weak—see Ephesians 6:4) and in another place not to embitter them (by being too strong—see Colossians 3:21). If a father has been a good nurturer and a good lawgiver at earlier stages, his ability to be a warrior/protector at this point will launch his children into a healthy and fruitful adulthood.

The Spiritual Mentor

This role is of primary importance to the older child as he or she moves into adulthood.

It is important that the stage of adolescence come to a conclusion. There needs to be a definite point at which a young person can say, "I am no longer a child. Now I am an adult." Traditionally, the event that signified this passage was the granting of the father's *blessing.*

Smalley and Trent, in their book *The Blessing,* describe the anguish felt by Esau when he realized that his brother had, in effect, stolen the paternal blessing that should have been his. "Bless me—me too, my father!" he cried. His anguish is echoed today by many people who still feel incomplete, who are still searching for their father's blessing.

Smalley and Trent point out that a "study of blessing always begins in the context of parental acceptance." They then describe the blessing as consisting of five basic parts: "It begins with *meaningful touching.* It continues with a *spoken message* of *high value,* a message that pictures a *special future* for the individual being blessed, and one that is based on an *active commitment* to see the blessing come to pass."[2]

These five things are more than ingredients for a one-time special event. They are elements that should come to characterize the relationship between a father and his children during the transition years between adolescence and adulthood. They express the father's acceptance of his children in ways that will affect them for the rest of their lives.

Unlike in biblical times, most of us do not observe a special occasion when the blessing is given. The fact is that our fathers either gave or withheld their blessing throughout the course of our development—and especially during adolescence. "Giving the blessing" is a good summary of the father's job description during this stage of his children's lives.

Unfortunately, the blessing is often conspicuous primarily by its absence. We often know we are missing something, even when we do not know what that "something" is. In his autobiographical novel, A *Portrait of the Artist as a Young Man,* the Irish poet and novelist James Joyce wrote about his self-imposed exile from Ireland. "Old Father," he said, "old artificer, stand by me now and ever in good stead." At this crossroads of his life, Joyce leaned upon an internalized image of his father for strength.

Parents in our culture typically have trouble "letting go" of their children, allowing them to become individuals in their own right. This letting go begins much earlier, of course, but it reaches its culmination when the children reach adulthood. Children have numerous ways of drawing us into taking continuing responsibility for them, just as we parents have numerous ways of holding them in continuing dependence upon us. When a father has done a good job in his roles as nurturer, lawgiver, and warrior, his children's transition to adult life will be simpler both for him and for them. It will be easier to let them go.

The spiritual mentor, then, is ultimately the source of "blessing" on his child, and the blessing is rooted in the father's acceptance of his child. What does this mean in more concrete terms?

One thing it means is that the father helps draw his children into the future. He helps them dream. These are not the dreams of night, but of a Don Quixote: dreams of overcoming obstacles, of meeting challenges, of making a genuine difference in the world.

At the same time, the spiritual mentor helps his children temper their dreams by facing up to their limitations. He does this in large measure by acknowledging his own limitations, by acting as a model. He sees, and helps his children see, the transcendent things in life; he also sees, and helps his children see, where he and they stand in relation to these things.

This comes through in the father's attitude toward the mysteries of life, all those things that are beyond our understanding. When a father can stand in awe of the unfathomable mysteries of life—the wonders of nature, the power of love, the realities of the spiritual realm—he makes room for his children to stand next to him as equals. When his children were little, he used his superior knowledge to answer all their questions. As they grew older, he may have used his authority to silence their questions. But now, if he is wise, he will accept their questions and invite them to join him in marveling at the truths that are beyond telling. He will invite them to join him in a humble sense of awe at the unexplainable—in a life of *faith*.

In most primitive cultures, and in many developed cultures in the East, the "wise old man" is revered. In our Western culture, however, we don't seem to know what to do with the elderly. We have lost the ability—or at least the patience—to listen to them, and so we set them aside, leaving them feeling useless and unloved. I wonder whether fathers could not start to reverse this phenomenon by being less self-absorbed and self-assured, and more willing to let their children join them in standing in awe of life's mysteries.

When Ellie, the youngest in the family, moved away from home, her father began to change his lifestyle. He played more golf, took more trips with his wife, and thought about winding down his career. But one thing did not change: He never stopped caring about Ellie.

Ellie sees less of him now that she lives five hundred miles away, but she is still able to talk with him on the phone about some of the questions she is struggling with. Dad is always an eager listener.

"I'm not always looking for answers," Ellie says. "I just want to know how *he* has dealt with some of these issues. He knows I don't necessarily want him to solve my problems. He can tell me when he doesn't have an answer. He knows I will sometimes choose to do things differently than he did when he was my age. He lets me be an adult. I think he's proud of who I've become. We are friends. I feel very privileged."

Ellie's father is able to acknowledge his limitations and allow his daughter to be an adult. He can stand next to her as an equal, and together they can look at life's great questions.

Fathers who are strong in the spiritual mentor role often struggle with the warrior/protector role. They are not *doers*. In fact, they may prefer to be seen as *sages*, above the humdrum of daily life. An overly mystical orientation can blind them to some of the things they could, and should, do for their children.

In my own case, I have many memories of my father sitting in his chair reading his Bible. For the most part, these are wonderful memories. But I also remember him reading his Bible at times when I wished he would play ball or do something else with me. Dad tended to feel that he had enough *doing* at work. When he came home, he needed to relax. Perhaps he felt that if he "got spiritual" and read his Bible, God would take care of the other things.

Still, in the spiritual mentor phase, fathering is more a way of life than a set of tasks to be performed, more a matter of *relating* than of *doing*. The father needs to address some new questions: Can he be open and vulnerable with his children now that they are nearly adults? Can he admit that he doesn't have all the answers? Can he listen to his children's struggles and simply share his wisdom rather than try to impose his will? To the degree that he can say yes to these questions, he will be able to fulfill the role of spiritual mentor with grace and ease.

This is the stage where the father can be an adult with his adult children. He has learned to respect them as adults, and he treats them that way.

When I left home to join the navy, my father took me to the train. It was one of those times that could have been significant, but it failed miserably. In later years I realized that my father was overwhelmed by emotions he couldn't express. He was scared. He felt like he was losing me completely. But we said little as we waited.

When the train came, he kissed me good-bye with tears in his eyes. How I've wished over the years that he could have talked to me man-to-man about those feelings. But we had lost touch with each other in the previous stages, and we had no foundation for talking about such things.

One result of my making peace with my father is the freedom to be more of a father to my sons. Since they are all adults, this means that I am not only repairing some things left undone in earlier stages, I am also seeking to relate to them man-to-man. The more I am available to them in this way, the more comfortable I feel in this role as spiritual mentor.

We have looked at four important roles a father must play in the lives of his children. As we have noted, each role comes into special prominence during a particular stage of the child's life. With the exception of the nurturing role, which is shared with the mother, each of the roles is a unique contribution that the father makes to the child's development.

Even though one role is prominent during each stage of the child's development, all four roles are important to some extent at every stage. Whenever one role is overdeveloped or used to the exclusion of the others, the children will suffer to some degree. If the father is not there, the mother may fill in some of the gap created by his absence, but she cannot *be* the lawgiver, the warrior/protector, or the spiritual mentor. These are roles fulfilled only by the father.

If Dad isn't there, and if Mom cannot fill these roles, what can be done to fill the gap? I believe this is where the extended family, or the family of God, provides an important substitution. Uncles, grandfathers, older men from the church—

these can help to fill in the gap. But no one can fully take Dad's place. He plays an essential part in human growth and development.

Of course, no human father has ever been perfect at performing all four roles at all times. Every father will almost certainly have one role that is dominant—the one he feels most comfortable with, the one that comes most naturally to him, the one he was most likely to resort to when the heat was on. As we look back on our own childhood, understanding our father's unique strengths and weaknesses will help us understand some of the strong and weak points in our own lives.

There are definite roles we needed our father to fulfill in our life. Think for a moment about your father:

- Which was the dominant role in your father's parenting style? How do you think his parenting style has added to your life as an adult?

- Which role, or roles, were most noticeably missing from your father's approach? How do you think this has affected your development? How does it affect you now?

- What did you miss most in your relationship with your father?

Record your feelings and impressions on pages 244 to 245 in the step-by-step journal or in a notebook of your own. Then use this as a reference while working through the next chapters. As we consider what sons and daughters typically miss in their development when their fathers are either physically or emotionally absent, refer to your answers and begin to clarify your own losses. I have used many examples to flesh out these ideas and help you identify the specifics of your situation.

We have laid the foundation; now we must begin the work of recognizing and naming our losses. Continue at your own rate. Give yourself time to process the feelings that return and use the journal or your notebook to record your thoughts.

With this firmly in mind, let's explore the times when our fathers weren't there.

FOUR

God as Our Model for Fatherhood

The Bible's portrayal of God the Father always goes beyond our experience of earthly fatherhood and corrects whatever weaknesses or distortions our view may contain. Let's look at the four basic roles of fathering that we described in chapter three—nurturer, lawgiver, warrior/protector, and spiritual mentor—and see how the Bible portrays God as fulfilling these roles. This is not to say that God is in any way limited to these roles, of course—they just give us a convenient way of understanding God's fatherhood.

Let's look, then, at some of the basic scriptural teachings about God's fatherhood, so that we can better understand what fathers do by looking at what God does with us, his children.

God Our Nurturing Father

From start to finish, the Bible presents a picture of a loving, tender, gracious God who cares about his children and extends himself in every way imaginable to assure their well-being. The apostle Paul sums it up when he writes, "What a wonderful God we have—he is the Father of our Lord Jesus Christ, the source of every mercy, and the one who so wonderfully comforts and strengthens us in our hardships and trials" (2 Corinthians 1:3).

The nurturing side of God's character is also clearly displayed in Jesus, who urges us: "Come to me and I will give you rest—all of you who work so hard beneath a heavy yoke. Wear my yoke—for it fits perfectly—and let me teach you; for I am gentle and humble, and you shall find rest for your souls" (Matthew 11:28-30).

The Holy Spirit, too, is described in terms of care and nurturance. Jesus calls him "the Comforter." He describes him as one who walks alongside us, consoling us and encouraging us. Thus we see that all three persons of the Trinity are portrayed in nurturing terms.

Matthew shows Jesus grieving over Jerusalem, crying out, "O Jerusalem, Jerusalem ... How often have I wanted to gather your children together as a hen gathers her chicks beneath her wings, but you wouldn't let me" (Matthew 23:37).

This is reminiscent of God's words in the Old Testament about the people of Israel: "How can I give you up, my Ephraim? How can I let you go? How can I forsake you ... ? My heart cries out within me; how I long to help you!" (Hosea 11:8). Surely these are the words of a tenderhearted, devoted parent!

Indeed, in some places the Bible uses the image of motherhood to describe God's nurturing side. Isaiah takes the people of Israel to task for believing that God has abandoned them: "They say, 'My Lord has deserted us; he has forgotten us'" (Isaiah 49:14). Speaking for God, the prophet replies, "Never! Can a mother forget her little child and not have love for her own son? Yet even if that should be, I will not forget you" (Isaiah 49:15). Isaiah depicts God as a nurturing parent whose love and care go beyond that of even the best human mother. He continues this imagery later, speaking of God's promises to his children. God says, "I will comfort you ... as a little one is comforted by its mother" (Isaiah 66:13).

Many of the Bible's most poignant descriptions of God's love for us are given in terms of the care and comfort a child receives from its mother. Does this call into question God's fatherhood? Of course not. It simply points to the impossibility of capturing God within purely human terms. The fact that God's mercy and tenderness are best expressed in terms of human motherhood does not mean that God is just like a human mother, any more than the fact that his protection and power are best expressed in terms of human fatherhood means he is just like a human father.

Scripture refers to God as a Father, to be sure—but as a divine Father, a heavenly Father, one who transcends human categories. God is who he is; the fact that our ability to understand and express his identity is limited does not mean that God himself is limited. And one area in which God knows no limitations is in his nurturing care of his children.

God Our Lawgiving Father

One of Scripture's most common ways of describing God is as King over his people. One of the most important functions of any king, of course, is to make and enforce the laws of his kingdom. The most obvious example of God acting in this way is described in Exodus 20, where he gives Moses the Ten Commandments.

But God goes well beyond merely handing down rules and regulations. Earlier we discussed a common weakness among human fathers who lay down the rules verbally but do not model them. When fathers *do* model the rules they establish, they help their children internalize those rules and develop their own values and morals. That is how God acts. He lays out the rules, but he does not stop there. He goes on to act in accordance with his own laws; he sets an example for his people to follow. He does not simply demand conformity to the letter of the law; rather, he makes it possible for his people to internalize the law so that they can live in accordance with its spirit.

Thus we see Hosea urging the people of Israel to "come back to God. Live by the principles of love and justice, and always be expecting much from him, your God" (Hosea 12:6).

Amos adds his voice: "Be good, flee evil—and live! Then the Lord, the Lord Almighty, will truly be your Helper, as you have claimed he is. Hate evil and love the good; remodel your courts into true halls of justice" (Amos 5:14-15).

Think about how a good human father acts in relation to a child of elementary school age. He clearly establishes the limits of acceptable behavior, and then he models it in his own life. When his child begins to test those limits—as any normal child will do—the father lovingly but firmly reinforces the limits, knowing that the child has not yet been able to internalize them and make them his own. As the father fulfills the lawgiver role, both with his child and within himself, he knows that the standards and limits he has imposed will become the child's own internal limits and standards.

In the same way, God says through Jeremiah that the day will come when "I will inscribe my laws upon their hearts, so that they shall want to honor me; then they shall truly be my people and I will be their God" (Jeremiah 31:33).

Paul explains that "the Ten Commandments were given so that all could see the extent of their failure to obey God's laws.

But the more we see our sinfulness, the more we see God's abounding grace forgiving us" (Romans 5:20). He later adds, "So we should not be like cringing, fearful slaves, but we should behave like God's very own children, adopted into the bosom, of his family, and calling to him, 'Father, Father'" (Romans 8:15).

Both Jeremiah and Paul are describing the fulfillment of the lawgiver role—imprinting moral standards and values on the hearts of the children.

God's lawgiver role also involves discipline. The writer of the letter to the Hebrews reminds its, "Let God train you, for he is doing what any loving father does for his children. Whoever heard of a son who was never corrected? . . . Our earthly fathers trained us for a few brief years, doing the best for us that they knew how, but God's correction is always right and for our best good, that we may share his holiness" (Hebrews 12:7,10). Many an abusive earthly father has told his children that their punishment was "for their own good," and his words rang hollow. When God says those words, they are different—our punishment from God truly is "for our best good."

God's aim as Lawgiver is not to restrict or control us, as it often is with earthly fathers who allow only the lawgiving role. His limits are for our good. We can internalize them and make them our own. We can respond to him even in his lawgiving role as sons and daughters, because we know he also has a nurturing role.

In fact, his nurturing side is an expression of his grace, and his lawgiving side is an expression of his truth. Thus when John says of Jesus that "we have seen his glory, the glory of the

One and Only, who came from the Father, *full of grace and truth*" (John 1:14, *NIV*), he is describing two aspects of God's fatherhood that are reflected in Jesus: his role as Nurturer and his role as Lawgiver.

God Our Warrior Father

The human father's warrior/protector role is one of struggling with his children in healthy ways, fighting for his children as necessary, and fighting within himself to stay involved with his children. How does God model this role?

From the very beginning of his relationship with man, we see God fighting to stay involved with his creation. When Adam and Eve sin in the Garden, rejecting his love, he does not simply erase them; he struggles with them to maintain relationship. Even when mankind's behavior worsens, he chooses to stay involved with Noah and his family. Later he does the same thing with Abraham and Sarah. The entire Old Testament is essentially the story of God struggling with his rebellious and wayward children, always choosing to stay involved with them, never willing to forsake them.

The prophets show God staying involved with his children long after the relationship seems hopeless. Even when Israel has failed to follow his laws, even when they have rejected his love, he keeps on loving them, seeking to restore their broken relationship. As part of this process, he disciplines them: "'I sent you hunger,' says the Lord, 'but it did no good; you still would not return to me. . . . I sent blight and mildew on your farms and your vineyards; the locusts ate your figs and olive trees. And still you wouldn't return to me,' says the Lord" (Amos 4:6,9).

Even when the situation seems hopeless, God doesn't give up the struggle. The judgments pronounced by Amos end with a promise of restoration, a time when God's children will once again experience his love, his care, and his blessings.

God also promises to protect us against our enemies, as David describes: "This I declare, that he alone is my refuge, my place of safety; he is my God, and I am trusting in him. For he rescues you from every trap, and protects you from the fatal plague.... His faithful promises are your armor" (Psalm 91:2-4).

Paul, too, speaks of our putting on the armor of God, so that we "will be able to stand safe against all the strategies and tricks of Satan" (Ephesians 6:11). We are in a life-and-death struggle with the forces of evil, and God himself fights alongside us.

Nowhere is this seen more clearly than in the account of the Israelites' battle with the Arameans. When the prophet Elisha's servant comes out of his tent early one morning, he sees that enemy armies surround the Israelites.

Panic-stricken, he runs inside to tell his master. Elisha, however, is not panicked. "Those who are with us are more than those who are with them," he says. He prays that God would open the eyes of his servant to see what he, Elisha, could already see: the army of the Lord himself arrayed on the hills all around them (see 2 Kings 6:8-23, *NIV*).

Throughout the Old Testament we see that God is determined to remain involved in his children's lives. He does not just sit by passively and watch us misbehave. While he gives us the freedom to make our own decisions, he never stops trying to guide us to healthy choices, and he never ceases to be ready to accept us when we return to him.

God Our Spiritual Mentor

It seems almost redundant to speak of God as our spiritual Mentor. Surely if any aspect of God's fatherhood is obvious, this is the one. Yet some important aspects of God's spiritual mentor role are worth pausing to consider.

The role of a spiritual mentor includes teaching. Certainly God revealed himself to his people in this way, and Jesus spent a great deal of his time on earth teaching. Beyond simply imparting knowledge, one of Jesus' primary aims was to help us to see, to understand, to *know* God himself. Jesus is the only one who knows God perfectly and completely, and in the context of our relationship with Jesus we in turn can understand what it means to have God as our Father.

As we saw earlier, Paul describes our relationship with God as one in which we are free to call him "Abba." Although we often think of this word as the equivalent of our word *Daddy,* the parallel is not exact. Professor C. F. D. Moule points out that "addressing his heavenly Father with exceptional intimacy, Jesus does not, however, take advantage of this familiarity. He uses the Abba address to offer to God his complete obedience. The intimate word conveys not a casual sort of familiarity but the deepest, most trustful reverence.[1]

The meaning of *Abba* does indeed include familiarity, but it also includes reverence and obedience. Moule suggests that the best translation might be "Dear Father," incorporating a sense of intimacy but also retaining a sense of reverence and awe that upholds God's majesty.

Even though we are among God's adopted children and therefore "joint-heirs with [Jesus] Christ" (see Romans 8:17, *KJV*), we still need to come into God's presence with respect and awe. To think of him solely as a big, playful Daddy is to miss what Jesus is trying to show us—that we are permitted to come into God's presence with reverence because of our intimate relationship with Jesus.

Another important aspect of God's role as spiritual Mentor is his involvement in our ongoing spiritual growth and development. Once we have accepted the finished work of Jesus on the cross and are adopted into God's family, Paul tells us that "God is at work within [us], helping [us] want to obey him, and then helping [us] do what he wants" (Philippians 2:13). Even after our salvation is secured, God remains active in our spiritual life, working in us through his Holy Spirit, stirring up within us the desire to become the men and women he longs for us to be.

It is important for us to see that God never relates to us in any one of the four fathering roles to the exclusion of the others. He has the unique ability to express all of them perfectly at the same time. Even when he is acting as a nurturing Father, he is also acting as a Lawgiver, a Protector, and a spiritual Mentor.

It is also important that we not limit our understanding of God to these four roles. He is always greater than our ability to comprehend or describe him. While these four roles help us understand human fatherhood as well as some aspects of God's nature and character, they do not tell the whole story. Let's look now at how these roles play out at different stages when our fathers weren't there.

Part Two

When Father Wasn't There

I would give you some violets,
but they withered all when my father died.
Hamlet, act iv, scene v

FIVE

Father Absence In Early Childhood

In the film *This Is My Life,* a single mother with two young daughters needs to be gone from the home for long stretches of time because her career has suddenly taken off. In a heated scene between the mother and her angry daughters, she complains bitterly that when she was unhappy, they were happy; now that she is finally happy, they are unhappy. If a child had to choose between a suicidal parent in the next room and a parent living joyously in Hawaii, she says, the child would pick the suicidal parent in the next room every time.

That is a profound observation. And it is true: Most children would prefer that both their parents be present in the house, regardless of how painful the circumstances might be. Even if Mom and Dad are fighting constantly, making life chaotic and miserable, most children—especially at younger ages—still want them to stay together.

What happens on the inside to a young child when his or her father is absent from the home? What is the result when the father roles are not modeled in their life? In this chapter, we will look at the effects of father absence on boys and girls up to the age of five. Our goal will be to understand how our own father's absence from our life during this critical stage of development may have affected us. As you read, listen and note situations and feelings that are similar to your own. We will assimilate this information once we have worked through the results of father absence at each stage of life.

When we speak of "absent fathers," we include several situations:

- fathers who, through death, desertion, or divorce, are literally and physically absent;

- fathers who, because of their own personal problems, are so emotionally detached from their children that they are virtually as good as absent;

- fathers who consider raising children to be "women's work" and so remove themselves from the children's lives;

- fathers who are present in the home and who are involved in their children's lives, but in unhealthy ways.

A father who is physically or sexually abusive not only creates many of the same problems as an absent father; he also causes other problems due to his violation of the child's personal boundaries. Children whose boundaries have been transgressed early in childhood often struggle all their lives with knowing what constitutes appropriate and inappropriate behavior in a given situation. They have difficulty becoming independent and establishing healthy relationships with others.

The most fundamental problem caused by an absent father—whatever form that absence may have taken—is the child's resulting inability to resist the symbiotic pull toward the mother. The child is frequently drawn into an extreme and unhealthy closeness to the mother, which makes it all the more difficult to become a separate individual.

A daughter in this situation will typically grow up living in her mother's shadow, always feeling that she and her mother are "just alike." A son in this situation will typically grow up always feeling like a little boy around women. When he marries, he will look for a partner who will mother him rather than one who will be his equal in an adult relationship.

Let's look more closely at the effects of father absence in the early years, first on girls, then on boys.

Pam, Heidi, and Lisa

Pam's father had carried on an affair with another woman the whole time her mother was pregnant with her, and he left home shortly after she was born. Her mother never really had time to deal with the fallout of his betrayal. She was too busy with a new baby and with the pressures of establishing a new way of life. Pam had two older sisters: Lisa, who was two years old when her father left, and Heidi, who was four. As we will see, each of these three girls was affected in a somewhat different way by her father's absence.

Pam's mother did a heroic job in those early years. The grandparents sent money to supplement her ex-husband's child-support payments, so she didn't need to go out and get a job until Pam started school. She was able to "be there" for her daughters during the early, formative years.

I once asked Pam how her mother described her as a child. "She always said I was the perfect baby," Pam remembered. "I needed my share of attention, but I never made extra problems."

Had Pam's mother been absent during these years—if she had needed to work, let's say, or if she had maintained an active social life outside the home—Pam's development might have been more chaotic. As it happened, she was able to bond successfully with her mother and to feel like the world was a safe place—as long as Mom was around.

When Pam started walking and talking, she and her mother had the usual run-ins, though they never got very serious or lasted very long. Pam couldn't afford major conflict. The absence of a sympathetic alternate figure to run to—like a father—made it very unsafe for Pam to stay angry with her mother. As we noted earlier, children in such circumstances often fear that their anger will destroy their relationship with the parent and may even harm the parent in some way. So they dare not hold on to negative feelings toward Mom. They put such feelings aside—they "stuff," or repress, them—so that peace may reign, at least on the outside.

Pam also had to repress her will during this time; standing up for herself against her mother's wishes would have been as unthinkable as giving vent to her anger. She needed a father to protect and appreciate her, but he wasn't there. Later in life, when she needed a strong inner self, it wasn't there either.

Because Pam was so dependent on her mother, she didn't know what it meant to succeed *as a woman*—she was still a child inside. In her mind, she had to be a man to be successful in the world since her mom wasn't considered a success. She had watched her mom struggle all those years and vowed she wouldn't repeat that cycle. Since she didn't want to be a man and didn't know how to be a woman, she simply remained a child and stayed with her mother. When I met her, she was twenty-eight years old, still living at home with her mother (who never remarried), and still in the same job she had taken when she graduated from high school.

The symbiotic pull of Pam's mother drew Pam and her mother into a *fused* relationship, in which they became, in a sense, the same person. One day a friend gave Pam a book called *My Mother, Myself.* Pam could never bring herself to read it; even the title frightened her. "It made me uncomfortable," she said. "I know I'm too tied to my mom, but I don't know what I'd do without her."

Pam has had several serious relationships with men, but she has always balked as those relationships have gravitated toward marriage. The reason, she explains, is that she always attracts "the wrong kind of guy." The first man about whom she felt quite serious turned out to be totally irresponsible. He could not hold a job. They finally broke up when Pam got frustrated at the amount of money he kept "borrowing" from her. By the time she ended the relationship, she knew she'd never get her money back, and she didn't.

A second relationship was even more painful. Pam had found someone she thought she really loved. Handsome and holding a good job, he was a real "catch." But he was always strangely elusive. There were mysterious blocks of time when he wasn't available, and the explanations he gave always seemed a bit contrived.

Pam discovered what was really going on one day when she was at lunch with a new work acquaintance. Her boyfriend walked into the same restaurant with another woman. After some awkward introductions, Pam's new acquaintance proceeded to tell her about the torrid affair going on between the couple they had just met—never realizing that the man was Pam's boyfriend. He later tried to patch things up with Pam, but she refused even to see him after that awful day at the restaurant.

A third relationship, with a man old enough to be her father, also foundered. It was this string of failed relationships that prompted Pam to come in for counseling.

Pam takes a very passive approach to life, but beneath her passivity lurks a boiling rage. I asked her once if she ever got angry at anyone. She thought for a while, then described a time in high school when she blew up at her best friend. "I was horrified by what I'd done," she said. "I was sure I had ruined our relationship. I almost drove her away—more so with my apologies than with my outburst."

People whose fathers were absent during their early childhood often describe themselves as "sitting on Pandora's box" when it comes to their emotions. They usually become increasingly aware of their buried rage as they get older, and it becomes increasingly difficult for them to "keep the lid on." The prospect of opening that Pandora's box, however, is terrifying; most people need the help of a strong, trustworthy guide as they begin the process of exploration.

Pam still works very hard at containing her rage, at keeping it out of her awareness. When I began mentioning *anger* as a topic we might want to talk about, she invariably grew nervous and changed the subject. She is only just now becoming willing to "dig up the box" and look inside.

Pam's oldest sister, Heidi, is different from her in many ways. Heidi had her father present for the first four years of her life. Among other things, this gave her greater access to her aggressive side and greater freedom in expressing it. When her mother corrected her as a little girl about something and Heidi got angry, she could take her anger to her father. Her will became better developed: she could oppose her mother without fearing that she was jeopardizing her own security.

Heidi's ability to express hurt and anger has been helpful in some respects, but she has tended to overdo it. Pam describes her as "always having a chip on her shoulder."

Her mother, in the same breath in which she says Pam was "the perfect baby," will typically add, "—nothing at all like Heidi."

Heidi did indeed give her mother all kinds of trouble. She got pregnant for the first time when she was fifteen. The father was a twenty-two-year-old high-school dropout who worked as a busboy at the restaurant where Heidi and her friends hung out. "Heidi always went for the wrong kind of guy," Pam said. "She still does, in fact. She's thirty-two, and she's been married twice. Both of her husbands were lowlifes. So is the guy she's living with now."

Heidi is looking for a father—and looking in all the wrong places. Her choice of "lowlifes" reflects her need to relate to someone who isn't too competent, who doesn't have his act together—someone who needs Heidi more than she needs him. She can't see what an obvious dead end this is.

The third sister, Lisa, is the middle child. More like Pam than Heidi, she still has some unique problems of her own.

Neither Pam nor her mother can understand the inflated image Lisa has of her father. She actually seems more angry at her mother than at him, as if it were somehow her mother's fault that he ran away. Lisa also feels that her mother abandoned her when Pam was born. Since there was no father on hand to fill the gap, she was left with an aching emptiness inside.

Lisa has never had a serious relationship with a man. She dates occasionally, but her companions are all just "good friends." Lisa says she likes it that way. In all probability, Lisa's relationships with men trace back to her idealization of her father. She cannot face the reality of what her father was like, so she maintains an idealized image of him—one that no man in the universe could compete with. It is impossible for Lisa to become serious about any man who falls so far short of her expectations, so she keeps her relationships with men purely at the "buddy" level.

"She's just one of the guys," Pam said of Lisa. "She's thirty, and she still dresses and acts like a tomboy."

We can see that their absent father has made a lasting impression on all three of his daughters. Heidi is still angry at him, which accounts for her dismal relationships with men; she gravitates to losers, who inevitably give her a justification for her anger. At the same time, her fear of being abandoned again drives her to get involved in one such relationship after another.

Pam and Lisa both have problems with their femininity. Little girls need a father around to help affirm what it means for them to be female. The critical time for this affirmation seems to come during the second half of the child's second year: roughly between eighteen and twenty-four months. The father influences this process largely in the ways he treats his daughters, being softer and gentler with them than he is with his sons. He does it by giving his daughters a feeling that each is "Daddy's special girl." Without a father present, the young girl's feminine side does not develop properly and may remain weak into adulthood.

Lisa has never really dealt with her father's abandonment of her. He is still her hero. She is the only one in the family who has tried to keep track of his whereabouts. Although he lives only a few hundred miles away and Lisa has seen his house, she has never actually made contact with him. Facing the reality of what he is like might destroy her carefully crafted, idealized image of him.

Father Absence in Early Childhood

A Daughter's Experience

1. She may become fused with her mother and unable to define her own identity as a separate individual.
2. She is often imprinted with a mistrustful attitude toward men in general.
3. She may idealize her father and, in many ways, want to be like him. As a result her femininity may remain underdeveloped.
4. With no one to be her champion, she is likely to feel insecure and unprotected, vulnerable to the world outside the home.
5. She may experience a deep yearning for her missing father that often intrudes into her relationships with men.

Each of the three daughters struggles in relationships with men, with work, and with herself. In each case, father absence in early childhood is a root cause of the difficulties. The ages in these vignettes are not absolute determiners of the consequences in adulthood. They are suggestive of the differences children will experience depending on the developmental level at which father loss was experienced. The effects of personality also need to be considered. Rather than getting locked into the ages suggested here, think more of similarities in experience.

Ron, Jerry, and Ted
Ron's father, like Pam's, left the family right after Ron was born. Also like Pam, Ron has two older siblings: Jerry, who is two years older than he, and Ted, who is four years older. Let's see how the dynamics of father absence affected Ron and his brothers.

During the first two years of life, the developmental process for boys and girls is pretty much the same. There is a strong pull toward a symbiotic attachment to the mother. For the mother, this attachment helps satisfy the well-known maternal instinct. For the child, it provides a sense of safety and security in a strange new environment. During this stage, the child—boy or girl—needs a "father figure" to moderate the pull of the mother.

With no father figure present, Ron was overwhelmed by the strong pull toward fusion with Mom. Without another significant male in his life—an uncle, say, or a grandfather—it was too difficult for him to withstand the attachment, to keep his distance as an autonomous individual. As a result, he became a "mama's boy," and grew up to be what is often called a "soft" male. This is characteristic of men who are not able to develop the aggressive side of their personality early on.

The issues that Ron struggles with are strikingly similar to those experienced by Pam. He, too, has kept the same job since he graduated from high school, despite the fact that he has been passed over several times for promotions he felt he deserved. Each time, Ron says, the guy who did get the promotion was either the type who didn't care who he stepped on, or someone brought in from the outside with less experience than Ron had.

Ron is thirty-two years old. He has been married since he was twenty-one. His wife often gets frustrated with him for acting, as she describes it, "like a little boy." She resents having to pick up after him as if he were a child.

"She's always on my case," Ron says. "It's almost like living with my mother. In many ways, they treat me the same."

As it is, Ron doesn't live very far from his mother. Their houses are only a few blocks apart. Ron calls his mother at least every other day and drops in on her at least once a week to see if she needs anything done around the house. This annoys Ron's wife, who claims he almost never pitches in with household projects at home. When Ron and his wife go shopping, they often take his mother with them. They do the same thing when they go out to eat.

Ron seems to get along very well with his mother, at least on the outside. Still, when he talks about her role in his life, there seems to be resentment below the surface. When I have commented on this, Ron has denied any hard feelings and pointed out how many things he does to make her life easier.

Ron's experience is quite common. There is a strong tie

between mother and son that appears very positive and supportive. But underneath the surface, the son feels controlled, obligated, trapped. Ron is loyal to his mother—after all, she gave her all for him, as he points out. It's almost as if Ron is repaying a debt to her. He feels as if he "owes her."

You might think that going through the rough-and-tumble of childhood would have been especially hard on a boy like Ron. It probably would have been except for the fact that his brothers were very protective toward him. His oldest brother, Ted, was a fighter, and he often stood up for both Ron and Jerry when they got into scrapes. Ron does not recognize how much Ted helped him; he seems oblivious to most of the difficulties Ted spared him from facing.

Although Ted is no longer around very much, the family still feels his presence. A career navy man since high school, he is seldom home. But he regularly sends money to his mother and checks up on his two younger brothers. Ron wishes he and Ted could have more time together. He wasn't that close to his oldest brother growing up, and now he misses him and wonders if Ted will "come back home" to live once he retires from the service.

The middle brother, Jerry, was two years old when his father left. After high school, he started working for the father of one of his buddies, and he has been very successful. He has received several promotions and is rapidly moving up the ladder.

Ron doesn't begrudge Jerry his success, but he seems miffed that it has come in the context of someone else's family. "It's almost like he's more a part of their family than ours," Ron complained. "When he was in high school, he used to go on vacations with them. It was like they adopted him or something. Jerry is more like a son to them than their *real* son—he doesn't even work for his own family's business anymore."

Both Ron and Ted, though they express it in different ways, seem to feel insecure about their manliness. Ron became a "soft" male; Ted became a "macho" man. "He's exactly the way you'd expect an old sailor to be," Ron laughs. "He likes to drink with the guys, tell dirty jokes, and talk about his 'old lady.'" It's not clear whether Ron disdains his oldest brother's macho lifestyle or envies it—or is simply baffled by it.

Jerry, on the other hand, does not seem to struggle with his maleness; he solved his problem by finding a substitute father and becoming part of a substitute family. As we will see in the next chapter, this has enabled Jerry to develop his aggressive side more thoroughly and to become more comfortable with his masculinity.

We spoke earlier of the phenomenon that occurs at about age eighteen to twenty-four months, when both boys and girls make their first step toward detaching themselves from their mother and establishing themselves as separate individuals. For boys, this is a time of attaching more strongly to Dad. If Dad isn't there to attach to, they will be drawn back toward Mom. Thus the effect of father absence at this age tends to be greater for boys than for girls.

During this critical period of gender identification, boys need a father or another strong male figure to identify with. It is as if there is a special "window of opportunity" during which the father needs to call forth the maleness within his son and to bless and reaffirm that maleness. The father doesn't have to be a muscle-bound he-man to fulfill this role. Most of what needs to happen will happen simply because he is a male and because he is *there*. Beyond that, the more connected he is with his sons, the more available he is to them, and the more involved he is in their lives, the better.

Studies of homosexual men report that many had fathers who were "critical, cold, impatient, and detached.... Fathers had spent less time with their homosexual sons in childhood and had been less likely to encourage their masculinity. Poor relationship with the father, and later seeking of male attention and companionship, are found in many chronicles of homosexuality: 'All through life I never touched my father. I was never allowed to even shake hands with him. Everything was at a distance. Everything was very formal. I found myself wishing to be close to him.'"[1] Thus father absence seems to be an important factor in the development of homosexuality.

Another common symptom of early father absence is a passive-aggressive approach to anger. This was true in Ron's experience. He was afraid to be openly angry with anyone, so he expressed his anger in indirect, passive ways—what is sometimes called "cold" anger. This passive expression of anger is very difficult for Ron to live with; it has a negative effect on his relationships. But until he comes to grips with his father issues, it will simply be too terrifying for Ron to be straightforward and direct about expressing his angry feelings.

Ron's brother Jerry was able to affirm his masculinity through his later relationship with his friend's father and family. He was fortunate to have found a substitute father to provide a healthy model of maleness; in a great many cases the substitute father is a poor choice, one who only adds to the damage already done by the absent father.

Unlike his brothers, Ted had access to his father during the early developmental period. He was able to successfully navigate the process of pulling back from his mother, identifying with his father, and then going back and making peace with his mother without being swallowed up by her.

So far, so good. When his father left home, however, Ted was very embittered toward him. From the beginning, he angrily refused to visit his father. Nothing his mother did, short of literally dragging him out to the car, could make him go.

Much of his anger was turned toward other children. Ted became a terror on the playground. He wasn't really a troublemaker; he was just always ready to fight with anyone, whenever the opportunity presented itself. Although the navy seemed to give him a sense of assurance that he was a "real man," his exaggerated efforts to be one of the guys betrayed the insecurity lurking just beneath the surface.

Both Ron and Ted are "at sea" when it comes to knowing how to treat their wives. Ron still acts like a little boy toward his wife, whom he treats almost like a mother. To Ted, on the other hand, a wife is simply one of the things he has to have in order to look like a man. He likes his wife and kids, but he doesn't really know how to relate to them. Interestingly enough, the fact that he is away on board ship more than half the time probably has a lot to do with keeping his marriage together. When he *is* home, he expects the house to be run like a ship. Housework and child rearing are "women's work" as far as he is concerned, so he sees little need to be there very much anyway.

Each of these three brothers—Ron, Jerry, and Ted—had problems becoming men. As different as their difficulties appear at first glance, they are, in fact, all related to father absence in early childhood.

Father Absence in Early Childhood

A Son's Experience

1. He may become fused with his mother, unable to define his own identity as a separate, unique adult.
2. He often experiences gender insecurity that leads to a struggle with masculinity; he may become a "soft" male, or he may overcompensate and become a "macho" man.
3. He may have a hard time expressing aggressiveness and anger and thus may become passive-aggressive in his relationships.
4. His longing for a father will often affect his work life. He may keep looking for a father in his boss, only to be disappointed again and again. If he does find a substitute father in a work setting, he may stay in a job for which he is overqualified.

So far we have seen that the father's presence, not to mention his active involvement, is vitally important in the lives of his young children—more so, perhaps, than most of us may have realized. His role only grows stronger as his children move into the next stage of life, the elementary school years, as we will see in the next chapter.

Take a moment before moving on and turn to the first question on page 242 in the step-by-step journal. Having heard the stories and descriptions of various hurting individuals, think back to your own experience with your father in the years before you went to school. Take some time to recall your feelings and impressions, the atmosphere in your home, and specifically your father's involvement and responses to you as a child. Record these thoughts in the journal or your notebook. Then let's begin looking at our father's role in our elementary school years.

SIX

Father Absence in the Elementary School Years

Starting about age five or six, a great many changes occur in the life of a child. Many of these are obvious: They get taller and heavier, and their facial features take on more definition. Their interests become more varied, and their activity level—though this hardly seems possible to already frazzled parents—zooms upward. And, of course, they start school.

Other changes are less obvious from the outside, having to do with emotional and intellectual development. These are the kinds of changes that are affected most strongly by the presence or absence of Dad. What happens to a child whose father leaves—whether by abandonment, death, divorce, or severe emotional detachment—during these later childhood years? What has happened to us if our fathers were unavailable during this period?

Surprisingly, most of the literature on child development has little to say about the father's role during these years. Perhaps this is because even fathers who are living at home and involved with their families still seem to be out of the picture so much of the time. This, after all, is usually the stage when Dad needs to work hardest to develop his career; he may be working especially long hours or traveling frequently. To the outside observer, it may appear that Mom is still the main—if not the only—influence on the children. The lack of research done on fathering during this stage tacitly supports the notion that fatherhood is nothing more than a social convention—that Dad has no intrinsic significance to his child's development.

But Dad *does* make a difference. In fact, the father plays a crucial role during the middle to later childhood years, and his absence during this critical period can have a profound negative impact on his children.

To see why this is so, we need only consider the enormous amount of intellectual development that occurs between age six and the beginning of puberty. These are years when our ability to perceive the world around us, organize our perceptions, and draw conclusions from them is growing by leaps and bounds. And Dad has much to offer his developing child.

In their early years, children typically rely on what is sometimes called "magical" thinking in interpreting reality. That is, they see no necessary, logical connections between cause and effect; anything they can conceive of seems perfectly plausible and possible to them. As far as they can tell, everything happens by magic anyway. That is why it is perfectly reasonable for little children to believe in Santa Claus and the Easter Bunny (why not?), or to assume that their naughty behavior yesterday brought about the rain that canceled today's picnic.

By the time they reach elementary school age, children begin to develop the ability to think concretely. The "magical" component of their thinking starts to recede as they get more in touch with cold, hard, bottom-line reality. They become better able to *categorize:* to recognize how specific bits of information fit together with other bits. They begin to sense the grand scheme of reality and to see where particular aspects of reality fit in. They also begin to *conserve* information, to hang on to things they have learned; and to *generalize* from what they have learned in one category to what must therefore be true in another category. It is an exhilarating process, and most children, if they are in a safe environment, will exhibit a natural curiosity that makes them avid learners.

This curiosity is not limited to book learning, to the kind of information picked up in the classroom. A large part of what children are learning at this age is lessons about life. The main way they learn these lessons is through their parents' example. When the father is absent during this stage, half the child's teaching team is missing in action.

When Dad is missing, for whatever reason, it looks as if Mom can step in and fill in the gap. After all, she can provide most of the child's most obvious needs—for food, clothing, shelter, and so on—with or without a father in the picture. And children at this age still relate to others one at a time. Even when both parents are present, children bounce back and forth from one of them to the other, rather than relating to both of them at once. This furthers the impression that Mom and Dad are essentially interchangeable parts—and that the child can get along just fine without one or the other of them if necessary. Thus, when Dad is absent, the child simply connects that much more solidly with Mom. He hardly knows what he's missing. Or so it seems.

In fact, however, the very opportunity to bounce back and forth *between* two parents is crucial to the child's later ability to relate "triadically," that is, to both parents at once—and this ability is crucial to many aspects of personality and interpersonal development, as we shall see in the next chapter.

We have been looking at aspects of development that are affected by father absence the same way in boys as in girls. In other areas, father absence affects boys in one way and girls in another. We will now look at four personal experiences of father absence, two involving girls and two involving boys.

Marian and Linda

When we observe young girls with their fathers during these elementary school years, what we often see resembles a sort of love affair. The father shows his affection in the way he holds his daughter, the way he hugs and cuddles and kisses her, the way he plays with her, even the way he teases her.

When Dad and daughter are affectionate in a healthy, open manner—and especially in the context of a solid relationship between the girl and her mother—the daughter grows up comfortable with her femininity, secure in the affection, admiration, and respect of the most important man in her life. She has an excellent foundation for relating to her husband someday.

When Dad is missing during these formative years, the daughter's ability to become an affectionate woman may be significantly reduced. Dr. Leon Hammer, a psychotherapist who specializes in female sexual development, notes that women who suffer from sexual frigidity in adulthood invariably experienced either father absence or a poor relationship with their father during their elementary school years.

During this stage of life, he says, one of the father's main contributions to his daughter's life is to teach by example how a man relates to a woman. He does this not only through the way he treats his wife, but even more through the way he relates to the daughter herself. Her father's response to her femininity reinforces her sexual identity.[1]

Marian was six and her sister, Linda, was nine when their father left their mother for another woman. Marian remembers seeing him only one time after he left. Her mother says he sent support checks for about five months, then stopped. When her mother tried to contact him, he was gone. No one knew where he went.

All her life, Marian has hungered for contact with her father. She has made various efforts to track him down but has always been stymied by his family's refusal to cooperate. Her story illustrates one of the patterns that frequently develops when a girl loses her father at this stage.

Even though Marian was the younger of the two daughters, it was she who most quickly and thoroughly became an adult in a child's body. She was "Mother's little helper," always doing the dishes and the laundry, cleaning the floors, straightening the house. Marian took pleasure in the fact that she was able to make her mother happy.

"I never really expected my father to come back," she says, "but deep down inside, I hoped he would. I wanted everything to be perfect for him, just in case—so he would want to stay."

Her performance in school mirrored this drive to have everything "just so." She was always a straight-A student. Marian does not recall her mother ever pressuring her to excel in school or to help out around the house. "It was just something that was important to me," she says.

Her older sister, Linda, became a source of problems for the family starting almost immediately after their father left. The more of a problem Linda became, the more

Marian worked at doing everything right.

It was while Marian was away at college that her mother remarried. Soon after that, Marian met a young man and fell in love; they got married a week after graduation.

"It was doomed from the start," Marian said, shaking her head. "I was looking for the father I never had, and I guess he was looking for a mother to take care of him. We struggled along for about eight years before he left. He insisted there was no one else involved, but he had a new girlfriend awfully quickly."

The collapse of her marriage was the final blow for Marian. She sank into a depression that nearly overwhelmed her.

"I never really faced what it meant to me that my father left," she told her therapy group one day. "I don't think I even knew what I was feeling. I just figured I had to be grown up and help my mom. I was probably in depression then, but what I've got now is much worse. I can hardly get out of bed in the morning. I can hardly do anything at all, let alone do it perfectly. My daughter has become more of a parent than I've been. Sounds like a repeat of my own life, doesn't it?"

Indeed it does. Like many people who have not dealt with the dysfunctions of their family of origin, Marian was indeed repeating the pattern of her childhood. One day someone in the group asked Marian how old her daughter was when her husband left. "I suddenly realized she was the same age as I was when my father deserted us," Marian said.

Marian's perfectionism was only temporarily masked by her depression; it was still the dominating feature of her personality. She had idealized her father, constructing a mental image of a picture-perfect relationship with him. The whole rest of her life was an attempt to make reality conform to that idealized image, looking forward to the day when he would come home and everything would be perfect once more.

Marian's husband never stood a chance against the idealized father image she had concocted. As far as Marian was concerned, he could do nothing right—a state of affairs she helped perpetuate by smothering his efforts to participate in the marriage.

"I was always after him to 'do something,'" Marian recalled. "But then when he did, I wouldn't let him finish it because I always felt I could do it better."

"Of course," she continued, "looking back, I'm not sure he really tried all that hard, either. When I'd step in and take over for him, he seemed pretty content with it. Basically, I think he was pretty weak, even if I didn't see it at the time."

This retreat into an idealized fantasy world is typical of women who have lost their fathers during the elementary school years. So is the self-fulfilling pronouncement that their husbands are weak and incompetent.

Another common way of dealing with the rejection of a father's abandonment is to escape into the intellectual world. This may be a woman's attempt to make her mark in a realm she thinks would impress her father. Marian, for example, was driven to maintain straight A's in every class she took. She was obsessed with her grades. As a result, she studied constantly, which was also a convenient way for her to ignore her emotions and the pain she experienced in the loss of her father.

Marian's older sister, Linda, responded to their father's absence in a different way. When a parent leaves the home, children often personalize the experience. They assume that it was aimed specifically at themselves; they tell themselves, "Daddy left *me.*" This seems to have been the case with Linda. Her immediate reaction to her father's disappearance was to slide into depression. She locked herself in her room much of the time—even while Marian was busily taking over running the house.

When she entered adolescence, Linda was surprised to find that boys were interested in her—surprised, because she was not much interested in *them.*

"She had a lot of boyfriends as far back as eighth grade," Marian recalls. "I know she was sexually active. She had to have an abortion once, and after that Mom made her take birth-control pills." Marian thought quietly for a moment. "She never got a bad reputation, though. I think that was because she always kept the upper hand. No guy ever really got to her. She's in her late thirties now, and she's never been married."

From Marian's description, Linda sounds like a woman who is angry at men. To her, they are all weak and worthless, interested in just one thing: sex. And she is willing to give it to them—but only on her own terms. It is not hard to see, under-lying her behavior, the anger that Linda must feel toward the father who, as she sees it, deserted her—or to imagine the crippling insecurity she must feel when she is with a man she *does* care about.

For Marian, the loss of her father deprived her of the opportunity to remain a child. She pressured herself to grow up too fast. Her sense of overresponsibility for everyone and everything around her, her perfectionism, even her aggressive intellectualism can all be attributed in large measure to the absence of her father during the elementary school years.

For Linda, the loss of her father made her angry at men in general and willing to relate only to men she was able to control. Her ability to control them only makes her despise them more—it proves how weak they are.

Linda claims that she is not angry at her father, that in fact she never thinks of him at all. At the conscious level, that may well be true. Her angry behavior toward men has done its job: It has blocked out the pain of her father's abandonment of her.

Father Absence in the Elementary School Years

A Daughter's Experience

1. The development of her femininity may be restricted, often leading to later sexual problems such as frigidity.
2. She may fantasize about her father's return. This fantasy can lead to perfectionism, intellectualism, and procrastination.
3. She may become fearful and insecure with men, having no solid basis for evaluating them and selecting a good man with whom to relate.
4. Her insecurity with men may lead to promiscuity or to withdrawal from relationships with males.
5. She often repeats the dysfunctional patterns of her mother's relationship to her father and to other men.
6. She may overcompensate by being excessively aggressive in relationships, or she may become too passive: a people pleaser.

Garry and Ed

A boy's identification with his father begins in earnest at about two-and-a-half to three years of age. He has successfully pulled back from Mom, has declared his independence, and is now ready to make peace with her on "manly" terms. This process continues through the elementary school years. It is an important part of his growth to healthy manhood.

It is natural for a boy, when he is young, to idolize his father. Dad becomes his hero. Dad can do no wrong. Ordinarily, this idealization sets the stage for the necessary conflicts of adolescence, when the son begins to come to grips with the fact that Dad isn't perfect after all.

If the father leaves during the hero-worship stage, however, his son can go through the rest of his life with a falsely idealized image of him. This can lead to intense insecurity and even self-hatred as the boy realizes he can never measure up to his image of his father.

As the boy moves into the later childhood years, he begins to see how his father copes with challenges, difficulties, and disappointments.

If he has no father to model himself after, he loses an important opportunity to learn how to face problems. He may even grow up under the delusion that there are no problems to be faced.

The father's role in his son's life during this stage is much more than being a replica of the mother. If he is present and actively involved with his son, the boy will be able to continue the process of defining himself as a separate, unique individual. If he is absent, either physically or emotionally, this process of individuation may be delayed or arrested altogether. The son will remain too closely connected to his mother.

Such boys often remain childish in their emotional makeup, even into adulthood.

Garry was six when his father died. His brother, Ed, was nine. Even though they were both in elementary school at the time, they responded in some distinctly different ways to the loss of their father.

It was Garry who came in for treatment. Initially, his complaints had to do with problems at work. He had continuing problems with disappointment on the job, particularly with his bosses, but also with other men to whom he looked for guidance. "I know they're not my father," Garry said. "But I need someone to look up to, and they keep letting me down."

His current boss, Garry said, was the best one he had ever had. "He takes time with me, teaching me what I need to know to do a good job," Garry said. "I even thought he might be grooming me for some important position in the company."

Garry was frustrated, however, because his boss never seemed to notice when he did well. "He sure notices when I screw up," Garry said.

"Why can't he say 'Good job' every once in a while?"

It became clear that, in addition to constructive input and training, Garry was seeking an emotional response from his boss that simply wasn't going to happen.

"It's always been like this," Garry said once. "When I was in school I always gravitated toward the male teachers and tried hard to get good grades in their classes. I guess I was hoping that would make them notice me and want to spend time with me. But it never happened. I've had several bosses who have been helpful to me and taken an interest in my work. Then either I let them down, or they let me down because I expect too much."

Garry's experience is typical of that of men who lost their fathers during the elementary school years. They look to a teacher, a boss, or some other significant male figure to take their father's place. It never works. Although these other men may be able to fill in for some elements of the father's role, the son is looking for more than a mentor. A mentor can give approval, but he cannot give a father's love or the special sense of identity that comes from being called "Son." The son is looking for a *father,* and it is impossible for anyone to replace Dad completely.

One reason surrogate fathers fall short is that the son has so idealized his father that no one could conceivably measure up. Garry eventually came to realize how idealized his image of his father was and how impossible it was for any teacher or boss to live up to that image. None of them was ever going to be perfect. None of them was ever going to be able to call him "Son."

Even so, Garry was luckier than many in his search for a substitute father. Several bosses had taken an interest in him and helped him grow, and no one had taken advantage of him. Tragically, some boys find an older man who sexualizes their relationship, leaving them physically and emotionally damaged. Others find that they have merely been used by men seeking to fill some void in their own lives, rather than loving and accepting them for themselves. When they need them most, these substitute fathers are nowhere to be found.

Garry's older brother, Ed, had more years with his father than Garry did. He was able to relate to his father during some of his elementary school years. This left him better equipped to express his aggressive side, both in his work and in his personal life. But the fact that his father died just as Ed was on the verge of adolescence set him up for ongoing conflict with his mother.

After her husband died, Ed's mother began to lean on Ed more and more as "the man of the house." Garry said, "I can still remember how uncomfortable Ed would get when people would come over and my mom would introduce him that way. He would almost wince when he heard the words 'man of the house.' And he fought against filling that role the whole time he was home."

Ed always seems to be looking for new ways to test himself. He drives race cars and has learned to skydive. When he is angry, everybody knows it. He is active and aggressive; he likes to make things happen.

Garry is just the opposite. He is passive, waiting for things to happen around him. He doesn't even like being in tall buildings, let alone skydiving. And he has never been able to express his emotions, especially his anger. This emotional blockage often leaves him feeling helpless around authority figures. Ed, on the other hand, is never reluctant to challenge authority.

The contrast between Garry and Ed also shows up in their relationships with women. Garry got married right out of high school and has been married now for more than fifteen years. He describes the marriage as "okay." He and his wife get along fine, Garry says, "but sometimes it feels like we're in a rut. We're both very responsible about family matters, especially the kids. I really work at being a good father. It's probably my highest priority."

By contrast, Ed—even though he is older—is very much the

overgrown adolescent. He enjoys being active and has a lot of buddies to do things with. His best friends, however, are his former girlfriends. He has had many relationships with women, even though he has never married.

The minute a relationship threatens to become serious, Ed backs off—always careful not to back off so far that he destroys the relationship altogether. He seems to need the female contact, but when things get too close he feels smothered and controlled. This is much the way he felt with his mother after his father's death.

Father Absence in the Elementary School Years

A Son's Experience

1. He may not learn how to be appropriately aggressive and often takes a passive approach to challenges.
2. He may idealize his absent father and often seeks a substitute—who is, inevitably, unsatisfactory.
3. He is often fearful of intimacy with women. His insecurity may prompt him to become "clingy," or it may drive him to keep his distance in relationships.
4. He is typically unable to express anger in healthy ways, either repressing it or giving it free rein.
5. He often has difficulty at work. He may expect too much from his superiors, whom he has cast in the role of substitute father. Or he may remain detached and unfocused toward his work, seeing it as nothing more than a means of paying for his amusements.

Ideally, the elementary school years are a time when both boys and girls become more secure in their developing manhood and womanhood.

They are learning about their emotions: how to recognize them, how to control them, how to express them.

Boys are continuing to learn what it means to be a man and to differentiate themselves from their mothers. The father is crucial to this process; only a man can teach a boy how to be a man. If Dad is absent during this phase, much of this learning is left undone.

Girls also need a father, to help them work out what it means to be a woman in relationship to a man. The father's presence and involvement will enable a girl to grow from a tomboy into a woman. Even if she is not physically attractive, her father's affirmation of her femininity will make her feel beautiful inside.

With this in mind, let's turn now to the second question on page 242 in the step-by-step journal. Spend some time thinking about your own experiences with your father during the elementary school years and record them here or in another notebook. Whether your memories are painful or joyful, it is important to remember and record them; for your father's profile must include both his strengths and his weaknesses. In my case, there are years I remember with fondness and years that I remember with pain. Whichever this stage holds for you, explore these years with Dad in confidence, knowing that ultimately it will bring peace, not turmoil, to your life. Let's proceed with this assurance and look at our fathers' roles during our adolescent years.

SEVEN

Father Absence in Adolescence

The well-known story *Pilgrim's Progress* is the saga of Pilgrim's dangerous journey to the Celestial City. He encounters many obstacles along the way as well as an array of inviting side paths that threaten to deflect him from his goal.

Adolescence is much the same: a passage from childhood to adulthood with many obstacles and tempting side paths along the way. It is, in many ways, a perilous journey and one that few of us would want to have to repeat. But if we are to arrive at our destination—healthy adulthood—adolescence is a journey we must complete successfully. And our fathers are essential to our success.

Adolescence begins with the onset of puberty, when many changes—both physical and emotional—occur with dizzying rapidity. Puberty marks the biological beginning of our full awakening as sexual beings. In fact, the entire period of adolescence is about coming into our sexual identities, either as men or as women.

For most of us, this is frightening. Even in a culture as saturated with sex as ours, when sexual feelings first stir within us, they are larger than life. What do we do with them? How do we learn to control them—to own them rather than be owned by them?

Without a strong rudder to help us stay on course, we can

veer off in one of two directions. We can repress the emotional turmoil within, or we can surrender to the whirl of our feelings and act them out in our behavior. Both directions can have serious, even dangerous, consequences.

To a large extent, it is the father who best provides the steadying influence in his adolescent children's lives. He is the rudder. When he is absent, the passage through adolescence becomes treacherous indeed.

It is also during adolescence that we fully develop our ability to relate to others as adults. We have noted that at earlier ages, children relate to adults one at a time, often bouncing back and forth between mother and father. In adolescence we become capable of dealing with greater complexity in interpersonal relationships. Specifically, we begin to relate *triadically*, or in threes. This makes it possible to relate to both parents simultaneously.

A triad—a group of three—makes family dynamics considerably more complex. Before, the child's world was a collection of one-on-one connections: mother-child, father-child. Now a triangle, a three-way relational unit, emerges: mother-father-child.

Family systems research has shown that these three-way relationships are the most basic unit of human interaction that gives us information about the people involved. For example, a newly married couple may appear to be very content with each other. But when one mother-in-law comes to visit, making a triangle, important information about the couple's relationship will begin to come to the surface. Handling the other two people in a complex, triadic relationship requires a maturity within each individual. Unless the adolescent has both a strong mother and a strong father to relate to, this fundamental interpersonal skill will remain underdeveloped.

The problem is obvious if one parent is totally absent. Difficulties arise even if one parent is present but weak or highly detached. If the teen is able to pit one parent against the other, he can relate to one as "all-good" and dismiss the other as "all-bad." But if the parents operate solidly together, as a team, the adolescent is forced to learn to deal with both of them. This is the main way in which the ability to relate triadically is developed.

The aspects of adolescence that we have discussed so far apply equally to boys and girls. As with other stages of development, however, there are also important differences in the way father absence affects boys and girls during the teenage years.

Jeanne and Amy

The young girl entering adolescence is already involved in a wonderful "love affair" with Daddy. When this relationship is healthy, it is nonsexual and nonthreatening to both parties.

As she begins puberty, new sexual feelings will begin to stir inside her. She will begin to see her father not just as Daddy, but also as a *man*. If her father is able to stay involved with his daughter and relate to her in a mature way, she will be able to integrate these new feelings toward her father. She will then be able to transfer her comfort with him to her relationships with males her own age.

What does it mean for the father to relate to his daughter maturely? Simply put, it means that he treats her with the same respect and ease he would show to any other person he is close to. Everything from the way he touches her to the way he engages her in conversation to the tone of voice he uses with her communicates, "I understand what's happening with you, and it's not scary to me. It doesn't change my love for you or my respect for you."

Men who are afraid of their daughters' emerging sexuality often communicate this fear in ways that make the daughters feel ashamed of what is happening to them and rejected by the most important man in their lives. One woman described her father's reaction to her as "being thrown out of Eden." She said, "He recoiled from me like I had a disease or something. All of a sudden he didn't hug me anymore. He wouldn't even touch me! It really hurt."

On the other hand, sometimes it is the daughter who becomes afraid of her new physical and emotional sensations and pushes the father away. It is she who no longer wishes to be held or touched. In most instances, this a temporary phenomenon that will pass as she overcomes her initial fears. Often the father can simply give her time. Or he may choose to address her fears gently but directly. If he takes the wrong message and backs away entirely, he risks becoming emotionally absent from her life—and both she and he will be the losers.

Jeanne's father divorced her mother when Jeanne was twelve. The breakup arrived totally without warning as far as Jeanne was concerned. Whatever conflict had existed between her parents had been successfully hidden from her. When they told her they were splitting up, she was shocked and crushed.

As the reality of what was happening began to sink in,

Jeanne's primary feeling was anger toward her mother. She became highly critical of her mother's behavior, pointing out to her all the things she "should have done" to keep Dad in the family.

This is a typical reaction for a girl Jeanne's age. In many ways, adolescent daughters compete with their mother for their father's attention. If the father leaves, the daughter may feel that he is rejecting *her*, and that it is all Mom's fault.

Jeanne's mother tried to be patient with her, humoring her suggestions as to how she should try to be "more womanly." But the power struggle never went away. It just went underground.

For years, Jeanne competed with her mother in an effort to win her father back. When he came to the house, she went out of her way to please him. She even flirted with him. When he acted uncomfortable with her flirting, she blamed it on her mother, who she felt was not doing enough to act feminine and make him feel wanted. Jeanne was unable to see that he was intimidated by her own emerging sexuality.

Jeanne looked forward eagerly to her visitation times with her father. Whenever those particular weekends rolled around, she seemed to come alive. She dressed her best and anxiously awaited his arrival.

"I was like a girl waiting for her date to pick her up," she laughed. "I wasn't consciously making our relationship into a boyfriend/girlfriend thing, but you'd never have known it from the way I acted and the things I talked about. I felt as though he had been away on a trip and was now coming back—coming back for *me*. We never talked about it, and I doubt he was even aware of it. But in my mind, I just *lived* for him for years after the divorce."

Somewhere around age sixteen, Jeanne finally gave up on ever winning her father over and bringing him back home. At about this time, she began to exercise iron-willed control over her eating. "My mom and I fought about it all the time," Jeanne remembers. "She'd say, 'Honey, you look fine the way you are.' I'd just ignore her. And when you got right down to it, there really wasn't anything she could do. I mean, she couldn't *make* me eat. It was one area of life where I had complete control."

Jeanne lost weight—gradually at first, and then with alarming speed. As time went on, she ate even less and exercised more. Her menstrual cycle shut down, and she began to look like a scrawny ten-year-old. When her weight hit eighty-four pounds, her mother brought her to our clinic for treatment for anorexia nervosa.

Anorexia is a mystifying and frightening disease. What makes a healthy, attractive human being decide to starve herself, sometimes literally to death? In many cases, it represents an unconscious attempt to stop growing. *If I don't eat, I won't grow. If I stay little, then Daddy will love me again* (or come back home, or whatever). One common factor in anorexia in young women is failure to mourn the loss of a significant male figure. Jeanne fit that description perfectly.

Of course, not all girls who lose their father at this stage succumb to eating disorders, and of those who do, not all become anorexic. Some go the opposite direction and start overeating. As they get heavier, Dad may start making good-natured comments about it, comments he intends as encouragement to lose weight. The result, however, is usually just the opposite: The daughter eats even more, since eating is her way of numbing the pain of the rejection she is feeling. Gaining weight is also a way of sabotaging her developing sexuality, which she blames for her father's leaving home—and leaving her.

Jeanne still sees her father about once a month. She always feels let down when she leaves him; her expectations for their time together are so grandiose that real life could never live up to them. Her father is still awkward around her, and they still don't talk about it. He is also still worried about her weight, but every time he says anything about it, they end up fighting.

Amy's father left when she was about the same age as Jeanne was when her father left. Her response was different from Jeanne's, however. It didn't involve any eating disorder. In fact, it didn't seem to involve any noticeable difficulty at all. From the very beginning, she handled her parents' divorce with apparent ease.

"I did withdraw into myself for a while," Amy says, "but I think my main response to his leaving was just to say to myself, 'Well, it's time to grow up now.'"

Amy was one of those people who was old for her age, who seemed to go directly from childhood to adulthood without ever passing through adolescence at all. Friends of the family always commented on how mature and grown-up she was. Even people her own age were fooled.

"I remember once when I was about fourteen," she says, "a guy who was visiting one of our neighbors asked me out. He was like twenty-three. When I told him I couldn't go out with him because I was only fourteen, he couldn't believe it. I had to get my neighbors to tell him that was really how old I was."

Amy didn't date much in high school—the boys all seemed childish to her, and she was very intimidating to them. "When I did date, I was terrified," she said. "I may have looked grown-up on the outside, but inside I was just plain scared. I had no idea what to expect with a boy, or how to act. My discomfort made *them* uncomfortable, so I finally just gave up on the whole thing."

Amy responded to her awkward feelings about boys by going into hiding, emotionally speaking. On the outside, she worked hard to act the way she thought a woman was supposed to act. But it was all a sham. She could only hope she was covering up the terror she felt inside, the terror that came from feeling she had no control over her life.

Amy was typical of many young women who lose their fathers during adolescence and respond by growing up too fast. Their inner lack of self-confidence, combined with their outer facade of sophistication, often leads them into relationships where they are used as sex objects. Sometimes this evolves into a way of life for them, where the only way they know how to relate to men is through sex. Statistics indicate that adolescent daughters from fatherless homes are considerably more likely than other girls to be sexually active.

There are other typical responses to father absence among teenage girls. When compared to girls whose fathers were present and available to them during this stage of life, they are far more susceptible to peer pressure. They are more likely to commit delinquent acts. They tend to be more aggressive. A much higher percentage of them will end up as single-parent mothers.

And they are much more likely to suffer from depression.

Adolescent depression is a serious problem; it is a prominent cause of suicide, which is the leading cause of death among teenagers. Teenagers' depression is often masked by high levels of activity. It may be dismissed as mere moodiness. To be sure, a high activity level or occasional bouts of "the blues" do not always indicate depression, let alone impending suicide. They can be warning signs, however. Both Jeanne and Amy said that depression has been a prominent part of their lives ever since their parents' divorces.

Father Absence in Adolescence

A Daughter's Experience

1. She is more susceptible to eating disorders such as anorexia or chronic overeating.
2. She may take on a premature and superficial "maturity" in which she looks and acts grown up, but is still confused and immature on the inside.
3. She may become fearful of her sexuality, either repressing her sexual feelings or acting them out with men in naive ways.
4. She may exhibit depression, delinquent behavior, problems at school, or greater vulnerability to peer pressure.
5. She typically romanticizes her absent father, creating an idealized image of him that no other male could hope to live up to.
6. She is unable to receive the "father's blessing" when she emerges from adolescence into adulthood.

Wally

As a young man approaches puberty and begins to notice the early stirrings of his sexuality, the person that first catches his attention will most likely be his mother. The attraction, while it is triggered by his awakening sexuality, will not be a sexual attraction per se. Typically, although the son will not have the same kind of "love affair" with his mother that a daughter often has with her father, he likely will feel a special closeness to Mom. His "love affair" with his mother occurred much earlier in development, and if the father was there during the early stages of development, his pull toward the mother at this stage will be different from the daughter's pull toward the father. To the degree that his father remains a strong presence in his life, his feelings for his mother will remain nonsexual.

When a boy becomes an adolescent, the father frequently becomes a restraining and even punishing force in his life. This negative experience of his father has its frictions and confrontations, but it is an integral part of the young man's developmental process.

In earlier years, the boy has consistently submerged his occasional feelings of resistance or rebellion toward his father. Now all that changes. With a new sense of his own masculinity, the son's assertiveness comes to the fore. The increasingly frequent collisions between his will and his father's are an important part of his growth toward manhood.

If the father is absent or is very weak or detached, he will not provide the foil against which his son can fight his way through to autonomous adulthood. Developing assertiveness with an absent father is like trying to build muscles by arm wrestling someone who isn't there. The results are invariably negative. They are also long-lasting.

Wally is an example of the damage caused by father absence during adolescence. He was an only child, and his father died when he was twelve. Though no one was aware of it at the time—least of all Wally—he had already entered puberty, and his emerging sexual feelings frightened him.

Wally never had the opportunity to properly mourn his father's death—largely because his father, just before he died, solemnly charged him with the responsibility to "be strong" for his mother. Wally took his father's words seriously; he never shed a tear after his father died. But he felt terribly alone inside.

"My mom was an emotional wreck when Dad died," Wally once told me. "Not me. I was like a rock. I really did do what he asked me to do. I don't know whether it helped anybody— especially me. I'm thirty-four now. That means it's been twenty-two years since he died. And even now I can't talk about him without crying. Look at me—I'm a mess."

If Wally's feelings toward his father were sentimental, he felt nothing but anger toward his mother. "I can't seem to be around her for five minutes without finding fault with her about something and then yelling at her about it," he said. "I guess I'm still trying to get even with her—as if it was her weakness that meant I had to be strong all those years." He sat silently for a moment, then shook his head slowly. "Strong— that's a laugh," he said. "I sure don't feel strong on the inside."

One of a father's most important jobs during his son's adolescence is to challenge him out of the passivity that often dominates a teenage boy's personality. This is no minor skirmish. The emotions of the adolescent male are powerful, even explosive, and the battle being fought is a fight between extremes: extreme submissiveness and passivity on the one hand, extreme assertiveness (with an occasional touch of "I-just-want-to-kill-you" anger) on the other. Living with a male adolescent, and watching the intensity of his emotions as he and his father lock horns, can be quite an experience. And if it is frightening to the observer, it is even more terrifying to the son.

A man needs considerable intestinal fortitude to successfully father a boy through this stage of life. Many fathers, though they are still physically present in the family, are too detached or too wishy-washy to stay involved in their sons' lives the way they need to be. They abdicate family leadership to the mother and bury themselves in work or some other distraction. Their weakness leads to many of the same results as if they were absent.

Wally was a two-time loser in this struggle. First and most obviously, his father was not there for him to wrestle with. Second, his father's well-meaning request that Wally be strong actually worked against the boy's ability to develop normally and become strong. When the powerful emotions of self-assertion and anger welled up, he felt he had no choice but to swallow them and adopt an outward air of passivity.

Nevertheless, the feelings were still there, even after he moved out of the house at age twenty-two. It was then, in fact, that he began to experience troubling outbursts of anger. He always felt guilty after these eruptions, but he couldn't get a handle on what was bothering him. He felt out of touch with himself.

A few years later, when Wally was married, he was shocked to find himself going through the same pattern with his wife:

angry outbursts, which she had done nothing to deserve, followed by periods of confusion and shame. Wally said he thought he could handle things with his wife as long as it was just the two of them. It was when either his mother or her mother came into the picture that things got out of control.

Wally came in for treatment because his wife said she would leave him if he didn't. The last straw for her had been an altercation between Wally and a complete stranger at a stoplight. The other man was driving too slowly to suit Wally, and after he rolled down his window and yelled an insult at him, they both got out of their cars to fight. His wife was horrified at the thought of what might have happened had a third motorist not intervened and cooled both men down.

Wally's outbursts of anger were all the more frightening to his wife because they contrasted so starkly with his more characteristic passivity. As it turned out, she didn't know the half of it. "She's always on my case about getting ahead at work," Wally told me. "The fact is, I got a promotion a year ago and never even told her about it. They made me foreman on my shift at the plant. But I didn't like all the extra hassles. After two days I asked for my old job back."

These kinds of work-related issues are common among men who lost a father in adolescence. Wally's unwillingness to keep his promotion was rooted in his conflicted feelings about authority. Often critical of his bosses, he was fond of bragging that he could do a much better job than they did—until he actually got the opportunity to try. Then he decided it was easier to fight authority than to wield it.

In some cases when the father is not available for the son to wrestle with, the son's drive to challenge authority leads him into delinquent behavior or drug and alcohol abuse. Wally experimented with drugs, but he never got caught.

"I sort of lived two lives," he said. "One to take care of my mother, and the other one to blow off steam. My mom never knew about the other part of me."

Wally went on to describe how he barely made it through high school. He regularly cut classes and had his girlfriend write excuses for him, forging his mother's signature. Though he frequently got into trouble, he was usually able to talk his way out of it without letting his mother find out.

Again, this "double-life syndrome" is common among adolescent boys who have lost their fathers. They are careful not to make waves at home, where they appear docile and cooperative. Once they leave the house, however, they become a different person.

The double-life syndrome often continues into adulthood. It is seen, for example, in the staid businessman who spends his weekends risking his neck in some dangerous activity like motorcycle racing, or in the apparently happily married man who seeks out the excitement of one sexual affair after another, or in the adult male who cannot make a commitment but lives life as a "flyboy," or perpetual adolescent.

The emerging men's movement has a lot to say about the young male's inability to become an adult without his father's involvement. The focus is on the absent father, particularly during the adolescent stage of development. A son may use high-risk or antisocial behavior to remain a child, much as a daughter might use an eating disorder. Both are trying to avoid the passage into adulthood with all its privileges and responsibilities.

It is these responsibilities that frighten the so-called flyboy. He doesn't want to be tied down to a job, a house, a family. If he is married, he will act as if he were still single. If he is single, he sets himself up to stay that way. Either way, the goal is to preserve his freedom to do whatever he wants, whenever he wants. But underneath the facade of freedom and adventure is often a frightened little boy who doesn't know how to be a grown-up. He is likely still struggling with authority, rebelling against anyone who threatens to put limits on him.

Later in life, when he stops to reflect, he is often confronted with the nagging feeling that he is still an adolescent, still trying to work out the tensions between dependence and autonomy, between submissiveness and assertiveness—still trying to arm wrestle with someone who isn't there.

There is, of course, no good time to lose a father. The beginning of adolescence is an especially critical period for both sons and daughters. Adolescence is the time of forging an identity, and the father plays a crucial role in helping both his sons and his daughters define who they will be as adults. Central to this process is the development of a sexual identity: being comfortable with what it means to be a man or woman.

Another important task of fatherhood happens at the other end of adolescence—when the father introduces his child to the world as an adult in his or her own right, when he imparts his "blessing."

Peter Blos tells the story of a young man who came to him for counseling about a major career decision. Two paths lay open before him. One would be very lucrative. The other would pay less but would be more meaningful to the young man.

When he asked his father for advice, the older man said, "Go for the money." He refused to discuss the decision beyond that. He would not even "acknowledge or consider his son's search for personal meaning and human involvement in his life's work. In disappointment and despair [the young man] exclaimed, 'All I wanted was my father's blessing!' Only then, he felt, was a free choice within his reach."[1]

The father's blessing is important to both sons and daughters all along the path of growing up, particularly when the child has nearly reached adulthood. Something special happens when a father can sit down toward the end of the adolescent stage and discuss with his son or daughter—adult to adult—the tasks and choices that lie ahead. When he does this, he leads them into the real world, away from the shelter of mother and father.

Father Absence in Adolescence

A Son's Experience

1. He may lose the battle against his own passivity. This may lead to such problems as drug and alcohol abuse, compulsive gambling, sexual promiscuity, and a general feeling of being out of touch with his emotions.
2. He may experience a diminished sense of achievement in school and at work. He may shrink from taking responsibility for his own advancement.
3. He may become a perpetual adolescent, a "flyboy,"

acting like a teenager with regard to sports, sex, or high-risk activities.

4. He may be unable to commit to a woman, fearing that she will control him or limit his options.

5. He may struggle with authority and authority figures. He may become predominantly passive, passive-aggressive, or rebellious in orientation.

6. He is unable to receive the "father's blessing" when he emerges from adolescence into adulthood.

Many of us never felt the power of our father's blessing. Some of us did not have fathers during crucial periods of our growing-up years. Others of us had fathers who were elusive or downright dangerous. All of us had imperfect fathers: that's just the human condition.

Take some time to work out your feelings about your father during your adolescent years, using the third question on page 242 in the step-by-step journal. Identify the ways your father was or was not involved in your life. Recognize how this affected you then and how it continues to affect your behavior now.

It is important to remember that peacemaking is a journey. Focus your mind on the destination, which is peace, and remember that this assessment of your past is only one stage in the journey. Lean on the support of a friend or someone close to you. Rest also in God, for "I am sure that God who began the good work within you will keep right on helping you grow ... until his task within you is finally finished" (Philippians 1:6). He will not let you down.

In part 3, we will continue our journey toward Dad by looking at ways some fathers let their children down. This part of the journey may be painful. We may not want to see the specific ways our fathers failed us. But for healing to occur, honesty is necessary. Remember that we are not looking for ways to condemn, but rather for ways to heal.

Part Three

When Father Let Us Down

The fathers eat sour grapes,
and the children's teeth are set on edge.
Ezekiel 18:2, *NIV*

EIGHT

Ways Our Fathers Eluded Us

A ll of us had fathers who failed us or let us down in some way and to some degree. Some of us had fathers who were absent through death, divorce, or abandonment. Others had fathers who violated us in some way, whether physically, psychologically, or sexually. Many of us had fathers who genuinely loved us but who nevertheless were imperfect.

What was your father like? Within this and the following chapter, we will begin to solidify our father's profile. Let's start by taking inventory of our father's characteristics and qualities. Try to be as accurate as you can, using the thoughts and feelings you have recorded up to this point as a reference.

My Father: An Inventory

The following inventory grew out of my years of experience counseling people who were struggling with relating to their fathers. Over and over again, people described their fathers using the terms that I have used to group the profiles within this chapter. Getting a clear understanding of your father's profile will be enormously helpful to you on your journey toward making peace with your father.

As you read each statement, indicate the degree to which it was true in your experience (a 5 means it was *always* true; a 1 means it was *never* true). Note that the two extreme answers are meant to represent just that: extremes. Try to avoid over-using the middle response—unless it is the only response you can honestly mark.

My father . . .

5 = Always
4 = Usually
3 = Sometimes
2 = Seldom
1 = Never

1. Had wide mood swings
2. Worked with me on my projects
3. Had to be "right"
4. Was rigid
5. Disappeared when problems arose
6. Was estranged from his own father
7. Embarrassed and/or humiliated me in front of others
8. Knew how I felt
9. Could express his feelings
10. Touched me
11. Was gone
12. Would let me beat him at games
13. Was reasonable in his expectations
14. Discussed things with me
15. Played the role of the disciplinarian
16. Launched conflicts that involved alcohol
17. Was gone because of work, church, or hobbies
18. Was someone I wanted my friends to meet

19. Sacrificed his own activities for mine
20. Listened to what I had to say

To find the father profile that fits your answers, look at the chart below and then turn to the page where that profile begins.

My Father: Profiles

Make two separate lists—one that identifies the statements to which you responded "always" (5) or "usually" (4), and another for the statements to which you responded "seldom" (2) or "never" (1). Look at the following chart to find the grouping of scores that best matches yours. Read the father profile indicated. Does it describe your father? If not, you may find him in one of the other father profiles in this chapter.

5 = Always 4 = Usually	2 = Seldom 1 = Never	Profile	Page
5,11,17	2	Workaholic	148
5,15	2,8,9,14,19,20	Silent	150
	1,5,8,9,10	Emotionless	152
5,7,16	18	Alcoholic	154
4,6,15	8,13,18,20	Tyrannical	156
1,3,7,15	13,18,20	Abusive	159
6,7,10,11	9	Seductive	162
3,6	2,12,19	Competitive	165
2,13,14,19	4,5,7	Idealized	166

Now let's look in greater depth at some of the common ways that our fathers may have eluded us, making themselves absent from our lives through overwork, silence, lack of emotion, or alcoholism. Again, I will use specific examples to help flesh out the terms presented.

The Workaholic Father

Work is both a readily available and a socially acceptable way for fathers to elude their families. Some of us may have had fathers who spent sixty to seventy hours at their job every week. Others may have had fathers whose jobs called for more conventional hours, but who nevertheless found ways to stay busy most of the rest of the time, whether puttering in the garage or workshop, sitting on committees, even serving at church.

Many times, the workaholic father will attempt to show love through giving money or material things. The father who is always away on business trips makes sure he brings gifts when he comes home.

There are many reasons why men become workaholics. For a lot of men, their job is the main way they establish their identity—the way they figure out who they are as a person. If things are not going well at work, or if they are not achieving to the level they think they should, they will often work harder, or turn to hobbies, sports, or other activities that will give them a sense of "being somebody." The tendency is probably deeply ingrained from childhood. It reflects one of the main lessons that little boys are taught: "What you want to be when you grow up," and how well you succeed at it, is the primary determinant of your worth as a person.

Mary's father was a workaholic.

An engineer with a major defense contractor, he had worked long hours for years in order to win the promotions he was sure would make him feel fulfilled. The promotions did indeed come his way. But each one merely became an impetus to work even harder to win the next promotion. Mary's father spent very little time with her and her brother while they were growing up.

Even so, Mary's father was extremely generous with money. As a little girl, Mary recalled, whenever she wanted anything, all she had to do was ask. She would leave her father a note explaining her request, and the next day there would be an envelope on the kitchen table with the money.

"It was his way of telling me he loved me," Mary said once. "In fact, every so often, he still likes to send me a check for five hundred dollars, a thousand dollars—for no reason at all. I guess he's still trying to tell me he loves me."

Even as an adult, Mary struggled to gain her father's approval for what she called "the feminine parts of me." She excelled at science and math all the way through school. For a long time she was convinced that she would go on to become an engineer—just like her father. "Dad was always proud of my A's in science," Mary said. "But I never knew if he was proud of me as a daughter—if he thought I was attractive as a woman."

Whenever Mary tried to ask him about this aspect of herself, he would choke up and change the subject. Then, a few days later, she would get a card from him in the mail. Once, long after Mary had married and moved away, she got one of these cards. Inside, her father had written, "I think you are a beautiful woman."

Mary was luckier than many children. Her father did eventually come to see that there was more to life than work, and he did make an attempt to respond to her emotional needs however belatedly.

Incidentally, Mary never became an engineer. She did, however, *marry* an engineer, who turned out to be a workaholic— just like her father.

The Silent Father

Some fathers are present physically but absent in virtually every other respect. They don't factor into family activities or discussion. In fact, they seldom speak at all, unless it is to punish. They simply do not communicate, living in an isolated, private world as if behind a locked door.

The behavior of such a father is often interpreted rather tolerantly. It is considered "too bad," or "a real shame," that he is the way he is. But he is viewed more with sadness, or even pity, than with anger. His children may be thought to have simply experienced a regrettable absence in their lives.

In fact, however, the effects of the silent father may be more destructive to the developing child than those of the tyrant or even of the physically abusive father. In our clinical work, we see more emotional devastation from this type of father than from any other, with the exception of the sexually abusive father.

I know that sounds like an extreme statement. After all, the silent father is not overtly destructive. His children do not bear the scars and bruises borne by children of physically abusive fathers. That, however, is precisely the point. The scars and bruises are all on the inside. And as far as anyone can see, nothing has actually been done by anyone that might account for the damage.

Paternal silence is fertile ground for distorted perceptions. Since there is, by definition, no way for the child to understand what is going on inside Dad, she is left to her own imagination as to what the problem is. More often than not, the child concludes that there must be something wrong with *herself*. What else *can* she think?

Sarah's father was an extreme example of the silent type. Sarah cannot remember ever having had anything resembling a real conversation with him. Sometimes he would ask her to get something for him—a can of beer, the newspaper—but for the most part his communication was limited to grunts and hand gestures.

Everyone in Sarah's family lived in fear of Dad. There was simply no way for anyone to know what was expected of them or what the consequences of disappointing his unfathomable expectations might be. Sarah remembers a typical meal at her house: Her father would grunt, and the rest of the family would be thrown into silent confusion and fear until someone managed to figure out what he wanted passed to him. Sarah learned from an early age that it was her job to please others including, apparently, developing the ability to read their minds to determine what would please them.

The pattern carried over into her adult life. She married a man who liked to talk—at first glance, the exact opposite of her father. But, as she eventually discovered, he didn't like to listen, and his talking left out a considerable amount of information that she was "just supposed to know." For twenty years she tried to please her husband, just as she had tried for eighteen years to please her father. Finally she simply collapsed under the strain. She slid deeper and deeper into depression, until most days she was unable to get out of bed in the morning.

As Sarah learned about the dynamics of her family of origin, it became clear to her that she had never really learned what love was all about. She had been taught since childhood to please those who had power over her; for her that was the essence of love. The predominant emotion she experienced was an abiding fear.

The Emotionless Father

I first met Brian when he came to counseling by himself for help with his marriage. "Let me give you the facts," he said crisply, "and then I want you to help me chart a course of action."

When I asked why his wife hadn't come with him, he said, "I don't want her going off on another emotional trip. She's already too emotional about things as it is. I just want to get some things straightened out."

Brian came back once a month like clockwork for three more visits, always having taken seriously the things we had talked about and having implemented them faithfully. The strategy we developed helped his marriage, and he seemed satisfied with how things were going. It wasn't until about a year later that I met his wife, Diane. She came to see me about a problem involving one of their children.

The first thing I noticed about Diane was that she didn't

seem at all like the highly emotional person Brian had described. I listened in amazement as Diane described to me what she had been living with for almost twenty years. Everything in their family, she said, was based on reason and logic. For example, the kids were not allowed to ask for things they wanted until they could present three logical reasons for why they ought to have them.

Diane remembered finding this somewhat odd, but she couldn't argue with the value of teaching the children to think things through clearly. And the approach had worked reasonably well while the kids were little. As they hit adolescence, however, they became increasingly frustrated with their father.

"They don't think Brian really cares about them," Diane said, "and I'm beginning to think they're right. I don't think Brian knows *how to* care about anything. When they were little, Brian spent a lot of time with them, teaching them things. Even our vacations were like educational field trips. Back then, the kids enjoyed the attention. But now . . . . well, now they want *more*. And so do I!"

As Diane talked, she began to realize that Brian was actually a lot like her father had been. Neither of them knew anything about feelings. It almost seemed as though they didn't *have* feelings. "I used to think my father was the greatest dad there ever was," Diane said. "But the more I see the same things in Brian that I used to see in him, the more I realize that I've always had this ache inside me, where I used to long for my dad to show me that he cared for me. He never did, and neither does Brian. I don't want my kids to grow up with that same ache inside."

A lot of men fit the description of the emotionless father. In our culture, boys are taught from an early age never to show emotion, and many of them learn the lesson all too well—to the point where they not only don't *display* their feelings, they don't even *feel* them most of the time.

Emotionless fathers may well be available to their children in playful and/or intellectual ways. A lot of them coach soccer teams and build science fair projects and help with homework. They are often excellent teachers when dealing with their kids. But once things shift into the realm of emotions and feelings, Dad shuts down and leaves—if not literally, then at least relationally. He is present in body, but unavailable in every other respect.

The Alcoholic Father
To many people, alcoholism seems like a fairly clear-cut problem. What could be more obvious than someone who is drunk all the time?

Yet it is often amazing what a well-kept secret a father's drinking problem can be. I remember Jessie, a woman who came to our clinic and said she had just learned that her father had been a practicing alcoholic all her life. She was thirty-five years old when she found out about it. Evidently her mother had been extraordinarily adept at covering up for her husband so much so that no one else in their small town realized what his problem was either.

When the family gathered and prepared to stage an intervention—a planned confrontation, designed to spur the problem individual to seek help—Jessie and some of her brothers and sisters had a difficult time accepting the fact that their father was alcoholic. They just thought he had been sick a lot when they were little. This new information about his true problem shed light on a lot of previously unanswered questions.

Most of the time, alcoholism is not quite this hard to detect. There are a number of telltale signs that family members can watch for—if, indeed, they are willing to face up to the reality of the situation. But secrecy surrounds alcoholism even when the alcoholism is recognized, and this secrecy causes problems. Children raised in alcoholic families learn how to keep things hidden—not just their parents' empty liquor bottles and embarrassing behavior, but also their own feelings about what is going on. This emotional suppression comes back to haunt them in later years.

When someone is an alcoholic, drinking gradually takes over his or her entire personality. In time, it becomes difficult even to talk to the person—you're never sure when you're actually talking to the individual and when you're just talking to the booze.

In our clinic, we regularly see people who come in for counseling for some other problem and lie about their use of alcohol. It doesn't take long, however, for the treatment team to recognize that when they try to "connect" with these people, something seems to be getting in the way. Even when they are not actively drinking, it is as though there is a wall around them that others simply cannot penetrate. Children of alcoholic fathers spend their lives butting their heads against that wall.

Many fathers, while not *addicted* to alcohol, nevertheless use alcohol as a way of eluding the family. If they've had a bad day, or if they're tired or under stress, having a drink or two becomes not just a convenient way to relax and unwind, but also a convenient way to retreat from others. Any possibility of meaningful connection with spouses or children ends when the drinking starts.

In a great many instances, the alcohol-abusing father also turns out to be a physically abusive husband and father. The incidence of sexual molestation is also markedly higher among alcoholic men than among the general population. What begins as a means of withdrawing from others becomes even more pathological, leading to increasing damage to everyone in the family.

The four types of fathers we have just looked at are all absentee fathers to one degree or another. The next three types are not. These are men who make their presence felt in the home—with a vengeance. In some cases, their presence is worse than their absence would be. We will look at tyrannical, abusive, seductive, and competitive fathers in this chapter; and then in the next chapter we will take a closer look at the harm they can do.

The Tyrannical Father

Children whose fathers were raging tyrants don't really need an inventory to tell them how their father went about distancing himself from them. The continuing sense of dread that they feel toward their father is all they need to remind them of his approach.

In John Updike's novel *Rabbit Is Rich,* a father who owns an automobile dealership wants his son off the lot and out of the car business. The lot, it seems, just isn't big enough for both of them. Harry, the father, expects allegiance, respect, and unwavering obedience from his son, Nelson. The fact that Nelson is a grown man makes Harry's power rather tenuous— and Harry's weakening hold on Nelson incites Harry to even more tyrannical behavior. Eventually, rather than continue to face the torment of being around his father, Nelson flees.

Tyrants are fathers who attempt to control other family members through anger and criticism. Sometimes their rage is directed at one particular member of the family, with the others seeming to escape. Interestingly, this is often experienced by those who escape not as a relief, but as a form of rejection; as unpleasant as it is, Dad's tyrannical behavior is the only form of attention he pays to anyone. Often the target of a tyrant's rage is a daughter who was "supposed" to be born a boy, or a son who is not "manly" enough.

Tyrants are very demanding. They often expect the children to carry on some family tradition, such as excelling in a sport or pursuing a particular career. The rage comes when the child does not seem to be measuring up or is not achieving quickly enough to suit Dad.

Fathers like this were often isolated as children, and they continue to be isolated as adults. They are sometimes, but not always, physically abusive. Even without physical abuse, the fear created by their tyrannical rage is more than enough to keep everyone in line.

Brett was raised by a tyrannical father. Nothing he did was ever good enough. His younger sister didn't fare any better with Dad, Brett thought, but she somehow developed a capacity for standing up to him, for arguing back. Whenever Brett tried that, his father would fly into a rage, and Brett would pay the penalty.

In high school, Brett did well in sports. He made the starting team in football as a junior, helped set records as part of a relay team in track, and could hold his own on the tennis court with almost anyone.

Brett had gone out for football because he thought it would make his father proud of him. No such luck. He tried to quit the team in his senior year because all his father ever did after a game was to criticize him for making "stupid mistakes," or for not playing hard enough, or for not making the big play at the critical moment. Brett's coach thought he had genuine talent, but he was frustrated that Brett wouldn't cut loose and just play the game. Brett tried, he said. But every time he did, the thought of his father's withering post-game analyses would tie his stomach up in knots.

In college, Brett majored in business administration. He didn't particularly care for business. He preferred psychology and sociology. Dad was footing the bill, though, and Dad was very clear that Brett was going to get his degree in business administration.

Girlfriends were a problem. Not *getting* them—Brett was intelligent, good-looking, and fun to be with—but bringing them home. He dreaded the scrutiny they would receive from his father. Needless to say, none of his girlfriends were ever good enough.

Brett's sister moved away as soon as she finished high school, attending college on the opposite side of the country. Between scholarships and loans, she put herself through college. When her father refused to attend her graduation—he thought it was a waste of money for girls to go to college—she cut off all contact with him. She still lives on the East Coast, but her father considers her dead. When she occasionally contacts Brett, he is careful not to let his father know that he talked to her.

The one act of rebellion that Brett ever pulled off was to run away and marry one of the girls his father disliked most. When the marriage failed after a year, Brett moved back home. At thirty-four, he still feels that his father is a domineering presence in his life, intimidating him and keeping him from even considering any more moves toward independence.

The Abusive Father

A father does not need to be an alcoholic or a tyrant to be an abuser. Like children of alcoholics, children of abusers are often surprised to learn that Dad had a problem. It would seem that abusive behavior would be obvious. But when abuse is all you have known throughout childhood, you somehow begin to believe that it is normal—that all fathers are like this. Or you begin to think that the problem lies with you, not with your father. After all, there must be some reason he acts the way he does.

Physical abuse is the most common form of a problem that can be expressed in a number of ways. There is such a thing as emotional abuse, intellectual abuse, and even spiritual abuse. The common thread is a father who does not respect the individuality of his children and who believes it is his duty to "whip the child into shape" in whatever areas seem deficient—by whatever means seem effective.

An abusive father is callous to the child's need for love—

perhaps because he is still reacting to his own blighted childhood in an abusive family. He may be so focused on himself and his own needs that there is no room for anyone else to have needs of their own; he is used to being catered to, not just by his family, but by everyone around him.

Dr. Adler, a character in Saul Bellow's novel *Seize the Day*, fits this description. He is a narcissistic, tyrannical patriarch who will not bend to anyone or anything. He cripples his son psychologically and emotionally. Indeed, the pain in the father-son relationship causes the son to seek escape in drugs, gambling, and sexual misbehavior. At the age of twenty, the son renounces his family altogether, taking the name Tommy Wilhelm.

But there is no escape for Tommy. The guilt he feels over turning his back on his family cripples him, driving him into a pattern of chronic failure in both business and marriage. Like many children of abusive fathers, he believes that the problem somehow lies with him, that he cannot obtain love (or even attention) from his father or from anyone else because he, Tommy, is inherently flawed.

In virtually every case we have worked with where the father was abusive, the now grown-up child remains convinced that if only he or she had been a better son or daughter, the father would not have been abusive—would not have *needed* to be abusive. These adult children remain trapped in a love/hate relationship with their father, still seeking his approval even as they shrink from his still-abusive behavior.

Bill's father stopped abusing him only after Bill slugged it out with him and prevailed. He backed down only after being knocked down.

In many ways, Bill's story parallels Tommy Wilhelm's. His father physically abused him for as long as he could remember. If a belt wasn't handy, his father would slap him across the face or cuff the back of his head. Bill has more than a few memories of being thrown across a room or slammed against a wall.

I once asked Bill if he had any happy childhood memories. "No," he said. "Only the beatings. That's all I can remember. That, and the terror I felt in my stomach every time Dad came home."

Bill was sixteen when he was finally big enough to take his father on. He flattened him with one punch. When he drew back his fist to hit his father again, his father ordered him out of the house. He knew that was the only way he could beat Bill anymore.

Bill lived with relatives until he was old enough to join the Marines. He didn't last the four years he signed up for; he was given a general discharge after striking an officer. But he stayed in the service long enough to learn how to drink, quickly graduating from alcohol to drugs.

His addictive behavior led to the breakup of two marriages by the time he was twenty-five. When he came to our clinic, it was not because he really wanted to change. He had to satisfy a court order requiring him to "seek professional help."

He was thirty-one when we met him. He had seen his parents only once since striking his father fifteen years before. His guilt, plus despair of ever being able to break the destructive cycles his life had taken on, had led him to attempt suicide several times.

Bill knew the statistics about how abused children often

become abusive fathers themselves. "At least I never had any kids," he said once. "The cycle will stop with me."

The Seductive Father

Some fathers are very seductive in their relationships with their children, especially their daughters.

It is important to distinguish seductive fathers from sexually abusive fathers. *Seductive* refers to a set of behaviors that do not include molestation. The key feature of a seductive father is that he is fuzzy regarding personal boundaries—both his own and those of others. He exhibits a higher degree of intimacy toward people than they are comfortable with, or than is appropriate, and often expects the same in return. In many ways, the seductive father is too open with his nurturing feelings. These nurturing feelings may be out of balance with the other aspects of his relationships with others, or they may just plain feel inappropriate to the recipient.

It is not so much that this type of father attacks another's sensibilities as that he smoothly manipulates situations in order to get what he wants. He expresses himself with a smooth emotionality that almost feels slippery to those not directly involved. The seductive behavior may be directed toward all his children, or he may have a special relationship with a particular child that is advanced through various secretive or furtive gestures, ways of speaking, touching, and so on.

The seductive father may be a weak figure in the family system, with the mother serving as the dominant person. This does not mean that every weak father is seductive, but many seductive fathers are weak in terms of leadership within the family. He is usually comfortable in the realm of feelings and emotions. He may be quite uncomfortable with his wife, to whom he is very submissive. The child who is the object of his quasiromantic attention feels special, but may also feel uncomfortable and embarrassed by his father's behavior, especially in front of friends. Something about the relationship just doesn't feel right.

The increasing incidence of divorce is producing an increasing number of "weekend fathers," who have a greater tendency to adopt a seductive orientation toward their children. The tendency works in both directions. Children, especially daughters, are prone to fantasizing about the "perfect father" and idealize the real-life father whose sporadic appearances in her life become so important to her. The father, for his part, may feel both a special need and a special opportunity to be his little girl's Prince Charming.

Bonnie was one of four children, and the only one who seemed to understand her father. The other three children were closer to her mother and tended to share Mom's patient tolerance of Dad's weakness and irresponsibility. Bonnie, by contrast, was his champion, quick to rise to his defense when others in the family criticized or complained about him. She was "Daddy's girl," and she enjoyed her special role.

The dynamics of the family split Bonnie and her father from Mom and the three other children as if they were on opposite sides of a fence. A vicious cycle was set in motion; the more Mom saw Dad as a problem, the more Bonnie tried to explain him and the more the family saw her as siding with Dad. Bonnie, misunderstood by her mother and siblings, felt understood and special in her relationship

with her father. Dad saw and appreciated the resulting align-
ment between Bonnie and himself. Thus the coalition
between Bonnie and her father grew strong, while the distance between the two of them and the rest of the family
increased.

Children, whether sons or daughters, raised by a seductive father struggle with their adult intimate relationships.
Either they allow the other person to dominate them, or they
push the other person away with an anger they cannot
understand or, in many cases, even identify. Either they
welcome closeness too much, or they become frightened
by whatever closeness exists in the relationship. Sometimes
they vacillate from one extreme to the other.

This is what Bonnie experienced, but could not identify, in
her relationship with her father as she was growing up.
By being her father's "champion," she achieved a close
relationship with him. But the relationship began to feel
too close. As she became an adolescent, her emerging
sexual feelings added to her fears in regards to her father.
She was caught in a push-pull situation—she valued the
closeness, but it frightened her. She wanted to pull away
from her father, but she did not want to leave him alone in
the family.

No matter where Bonnie was in her relationship with her
father, she ended up feeling uncomfortable. As an adult,
she has not been able to find a comfortable way to relate to
the men in her life either. She tries to achieve intimacy,
but if she succeeds, she backs off. What she didn't realize
before she came for counseling was that her father's seductive behavior played a major part in her confusion.

The Competitive Father

The competitive father is often experienced as "macho." He is in many ways the opposite of the father we just discussed.

This type of father was frequently abandoned by his own father, prompting him to overcompensate in his attempts to be manly. His male identity is quite fragile and must be protected at all costs, even from his own children. This often shows up in the way he plays with them: There must always be a winner and a loser, and the winner must always be Dad.

Daughters of competitive fathers often feel the contempt that these fathers seem to have for women. Even though the father may try to behave appropriately toward women, there is an undercurrent of hidden hostility that eventually comes through. Some therapists believe that this hostility is centered on the man's own mother; at a deep, unconscious level he blames her for his father's leaving, even though he is not aware of these feelings. Denial becomes a way of life, not only for the competitive father, but also for everyone else in the family.

Typically, the children of competitive, overbearing fathers carry a basic feeling of unhappiness, depression, and hopelessness. Many simply give up on their families and bide their time until they can get away. Others let the pressure build up inside them like a volcano, until they finally explode in a torrent of resentment and anger.

Tom was the embodiment of everything that comes to mind when you think of "machismo." He had strong opinions about everything, which he expressed without concern for others' feelings. These opinions prominently included the belief that a wide range of other types of people—especially women—needed to be kept in their place.

Tom's family entered treatment because of one of the sons, who was, as Tom put it, "wimping out on me." The other son, on the other hand, was becoming increasingly belligerent. The warfare among Tom's children was becoming intense. Even so, Tom himself was not particularly interested in getting help. He didn't think he needed any. He only came to sessions because full family participation was a requirement of the clinic.

It didn't take long for Tom's basic disposition to show itself. Tom always competed with his children. In fact, he competed with anyone in the family who even appeared to differ with him on any point. No matter what anyone else in the family said, Tom took it as a challenge to his position and defended himself passionately. Had the therapist not intervened—in effect, she told Tom to shut up—no one else would have ever been heard from. Tom would have beaten them down with his arguments and intimidated them into complete silence.

Are there then no perfect fathers? Unfortunately, there are not. Our fathers all made mistakes, just as we too make mistakes if we are parents. For some people, this reality is too hard to bear. Whatever their fathers' faults, they are blind to them. They prefer to invent a father to worship, rather than relate to the father they actually have.

The Idealized Father
It is common for children whose fathers have left the home or died to create a fictional Dad to stand in place of the absent one. Strangely, it is not uncommon for children whose fathers

eluded or mistreated them in the various ways we have discussed in this chapter to do the same thing. They would rather admire an imaginary father than deal with the real, defective one they live with.

If your father's pattern on the Inventory matches the pattern of the idealized father, you may be dealing with an image rather than with reality. The tendency to idealize a father is often passed on to us, often by our own father, who may have idealized his father.

Children who idealize Dad will vehemently express respect and admiration for him. Nevertheless, they are keeping Dad at a distance. They are not dealing with the real person, but with a character devised in their own imagination. They deny the existence of any negative or imperfect aspects of Dad's character or personality and focus only on positive traits—which may be real or imagined. A good test of whether we are idealizing our father is to look at how we react when someone suggests Dad may have been inadequate in some way. An angry, defensive reaction is symptomatic of idealization.

One result of idealizing Dad is a sense of guilt over our own inadequacy. We measure ourselves against our picture of our father, and inevitably we fall short. It then becomes a vicious cycle, because every time we fall short, we elevate Dad to an even higher pedestal.

Sherri's father died when she was twelve. When I asked her what she remembered about him, she smiled and described a virtuous, heroic, utterly perfect human being. I pressed her for any less-than-perfect aspects he may have had, but the more I did, the more positive traits she recited. The tables were turned when we discussed her mother. Sherri had nothing good whatsoever to say about her

What Sherri was doing is called "splitting." It represents our tendency to make one person all-good and the other person all-bad. Little children do it all the time; it's a natural part of the process of emotional development. When adults practice splitting, however, it can cause trouble.

In her strong attachment to the too-good father, Sherri was setting herself up for some serious problems. To preserve her image of her father, she had to explain away his shortcomings as inadequacies in someone else. First it was her mother: Dad was all-good; Mom was all-bad. Eventually Sherri attached this badness to herself as well. Her idealized view of her father was the driving force behind a perfectionism that enslaved her.

Sherri's unrealistic view of her father also led her to adopt unrealistic expectations of her husband. Walt was a fine man and a good husband, but Sherri had come to see him as hopelessly inadequate. She resented his weaknesses and believed there was almost nothing that she could not do better than he could. She laughed at the very thought of comparing Walt to her father.

Without realizing it, Sherri had cast her marriage in the same mold as she had her parents—seeing one person as the repository of all that is good, and the other as the embodiment of all that is bad. No matter what issues we discussed, her inevitable refrain was that Walt had to "fix himself" before they could hope to have a successful marriage. Until Sherri becomes comfortable with the untidiness of human reality— that all of us have both good and bad qualities, but that all of us are unique and valuable just the same—she will be imprisoned by her distorted view of life.

Think about your own mental image of your father. If the picture you carry of him seems too good to be true, there is a good chance that it *isn't* true. I am certainly not advocating that we set out to adopt a harshly negative view of our fathers—or of anyone else, for that matter. It is entirely right for us to view our parents with charity and with respect. But we also need to adopt a *realistic* view of our parents, acknowledging both their strengths and their weaknesses. Only when we see them as they truly are can we relate to them on a solid footing of reality. Only then are we free to grow up and become healthy adults ourselves.

The Good-Enough Father

All of our fathers are imperfect, at least to some degree. The fact is that, like us, few of our fathers had good models or training for what it means to be healthy, effective parents. We need not find this particularly shocking or dismaying. It is simply part of the human condition.

No one is perfect. Everyone makes mistakes. Everyone operates from a base of wisdom and understanding that is less than complete. As we become parents, we will fall into this category, too. Realizing that we are imperfect parents humbles us and forces us to look for wisdom beyond ourselves and our own experience.

The goal of any parent is to be "good enough." Our children will cut us a lot of slack, especially when they know we love them and are really working at being present in their lives. Accepting imperfections in our relationships is a major step in our coming to terms with ourselves as well as with our father.

My father died when I was twenty-two years old. I remember the day my own son turned twenty-two. It suddenly dawned on me: "I don't have any model for what to do now." I simply had no personal experience of what a father-son relationship looked like once the son became twenty-two. Then I remembered that my father's father had also died when he was quite young. My father, too, had to "fly by instruments" for a long time.

Many men have had this experience. One friend of mine describes it as feeling like a dachshund running in deep snow: The harder he tries to move forward, the deeper he digs his way into a hole.

Imperfection is something we have to accept. Cruelty, however, is not. The line between the two is sometimes hard to distinguish. Was the damage Dad inflicted intentional or accidental? Did Dad know any better way to act? How serious were the effects of Dad's behavior?

In the next chapter we will look at fathers who are dangerous. Whether they are intentionally cruel or ignorantly destructive, they damage their children. It is not pleasant to read about these fathers. But even if we discover that our father was dangerous, we can still find reconciliation and peace. On our journey toward Dad, we must wind through the forest to reach the light. The forest is dense and deep, but it will not destroy us if we continue on the journey.

NINE

Doubly Dangerous Fathers

Woody Allen once said, "Ninety percent of success is just showing up."

As we have seen, we can suffer a wide range of consequences from the absence of our father, whether this absence is literal—resulting from death, desertion, or divorce—or emotional, where the father is there but not there, present in the home but so detached from his children that he might as well not be there at all. Particularly when children are young, the father can make a significant contribution to their development simply by being male and by being present.

Of course there is more to being a father than "just showing up." On the positive side, there are many things a father needs to bring to his children, many ways he needs to actively invest himself in their lives, if he is to succeed. And on the negative side, there are ways in which fathers can seriously damage their children through the harmful and destructive ways they relate to them.

In the previous chapter we looked at some fathers who were physically, sexually, or psychologically abusive. In many cases, their children would have been better off if their fathers had been absent. Indeed, such children have suffered doubly; not only were they deprived of the presence of the healthy, supportive father who should have been there, but they also sustained the damage inflicted by the abusive father who *was* there. Thus they experienced some of the same problems as children whose fathers were absent, and additional consequences besides.

In this chapter, we'll take a closer look at four types of fathers whose presence harms their children.

The Physically Abusive Father

Virginia's father was an alcoholic. He was also, in the parlance of alcoholics, a "mean drunk." You could count on it: When he drank, someone was going to get hurt. Often that someone was a member of his family.

Virginia felt trapped. She wanted to run away, and she almost did several times. But fear of what would happen when she returned stopped her. When she was sixteen she unsuccessfully tried to commit suicide by taking an overdose of her mother's pain medication.

Even though she felt trapped, part of Virginia's response to her father's abuse was increased loyalty to her mother and sister. More than once she stepped in to protect her mother from her father, only to receive the blow that had been meant for her mother. She never went to college, because she didn't want to leave her younger sister unprotected. It wasn't until her father died, when she was twenty-three, that Virginia finally felt free to pursue her own life.

Other children in Virginia's situation respond in precisely the opposite way: They leave home as soon as possible. As far as they are concerned, other family members can look after themselves as best they can—they just want to get out. It is not uncommon for daughters of abusive fathers to rush into marriage as a way to escape their violent home life. In a large number of cases, however, these women gravitate to husbands who are just as abusive as their fathers.

Virginia met her future husband, Les, soon after her father died, and they were married less than six months later. Virginia insists there were no signs of trouble before the wedding. It wasn't long, however, before she realized that a terrible pattern was repeating itself in her life.

"I can't count the number of times I grabbed the kids and ran off to the shelter," she said, referring to a local "safe house" established for battered wives. "Les would always come around a few days later and say he was sorry for what he had done, and we'd pack up and go back home. He always swore he'd never do it again. But he always did."

Virginia was trapped in a cycle of violence that didn't begin with Les. It began earlier, in her family of origin—and in his. I never got to talk to Les directly, but Virginia shared with me what his home life had been like. Les was the oldest child, and his father was especially demanding of him. When anything went wrong, his father would grab whatever was close at hand and start hitting Les with it. One time he grabbed a two-by-four and knocked Les out cold.

Here, then, were two abused people who, in their attempt to avoid what they had experienced as children, unwittingly flung themselves into a situation where the pattern repeated itself. The only way out was for both of them to go back and work through the pain, guilt, and fear of their childhood traumas.

Although public awareness of child abuse has increased dramatically in recent years, the actual number of abused children is still unknown. The number of reported cases has risen steadily since the mid-seventies. Most experts believe these statistics still represent only the tip of the iceberg.

Abusive fathers cause many of the same problems as absent fathers. In both cases, the child is thrown back upon the mother as the sole source of support. In abuse situations, however, Mom is often seen less as a protector than as a coconspirator, one who either cannot or will not put a stop to the terror. Thus the child is driven to forsake being a child and to learn how to protect himself.

Unlike children of absent fathers, children of abusive fathers do not idealize them. Instead, they live in constant fear of them and their destructive behavior. This fearful attitude follows them into adulthood and colors their entire outlook on life. When you talk with Virginia, for example, you can see it in her eyes: a hypervigilance, as if she is constantly scanning the horizon, looking for hidden danger.

There is an extraordinarily high likelihood that daughters of abusive fathers will marry abusive husbands, and that sons of abusive fathers will become abusers themselves. This repetition of the abuse cycle is not consciously and deliberately chosen. Rather, it represents a powerful unconscious drive to resolve the pain of childhood abuse.

Some children—especially boys, with their greater innate aggressiveness—grow up consumed with unconscious rage that they seek to out on someone else. Others—especially girls—become extremely passive. Their feelings of victimization are so strong that being a victim becomes their identity, their primary way of relating to the world. They virtually invite someone's rage to be directed at them.

In fact, the pain of childhood abuse can be resolved only in the context of both parents—the one who did the abusing, and the one who in some way allowed it to occur. For obvious reasons, this often seems impossible; there is understandable fear of the abusive parent and often bitterness toward the "enabling" parent. But it can be done, as we will see in a later chapter.

Additional Losses from the Abusive Father

1. The child is pushed back toward the mother, even more than with the absent father. As a young adult, the abused person may feel unable to leave home.
2. The child develops a fearful posture toward all of life.
3. The cycle of abuse is often carried over into the next generation.
4. Common symptoms include academic problems, dropping out of school, running away, suicide.
5. As an adult, the abused person often becomes hypervigilant, consumed with anxiety about real or imagined danger.
6. The abused person is typically fearful of anger, both in himself and in others.
7. In adult life, the abused person is commonly subject to bouts of serious depression.

The Molesting Father

Fathers who sexually molest their children cause them all the same problems as fathers who are physically abusive—and more. The damage to the child's image of herself goes much deeper. The child's boundaries have been violated in a way that leaves her feeling almost totally defenseless. As an adult, the victim of childhood sexual abuse searches frantically for someone or something to help her make sense of life by setting limits for her. It is as if she feels she does not have the right to set limits for herself.

The outworkings of childhood sexual abuse typically go in one of two directions. Some children grow up to be promiscuous adolescents and adults. They continue to act out a sexuality without boundaries, a life that acknowledges no limits. Why should there—how *could* there—be any limits, now that the most sacred boundary of all has been trampled by the one person they should have been able to trust the most? This unconscious question seems to drive their behavior.

Others who have been molested spend their lives obsessively creating artificial boundaries designed to keep the world at a safe distance. They may, for example, become rigidly controlled in their expression of emotion. Quite often they turn to food. It is as if the layer of fat caused by their overeating serves as a shield against the outside world.

Not every woman with a weight problem was sexually abused in childhood, of course, but it is quite common for women who were molested in childhood to become overweight as an unconscious way to keep men at a distance. This dynamic often reveals itself when they go on a diet and start to lose weight. Suddenly confronted with fears about their sexuality and with painful memories, they may quickly go back to overeating.

Debbie came to our clinic because she had started having flashbacks to some frightening memories. In time she was able to clarify her recollections and acknowledge that her father had repeatedly molested her between the ages of twelve and fourteen. The pattern actually began when she was even younger—about nine. Her father would share secrets with her, coming into her room and talking with her alone, telling her things that he said "are only for you and me to know." When he started touching her, she was confused. On the one hand, it frightened her; on the other hand, it felt pleasurable.

The abuse stopped when Debbie turned fourteen, apparently because her father transferred his attentions to Debbie's younger sister. At the time, Debbie didn't know why he stopped. She just lived in terror that he might start again.

When Debbie got a boyfriend at about age sixteen, her father went on a rampage. He accused her of being sexually active and demanded that the boy come to the house for questioning. By the time her father was finished raging at her boyfriend, Debbie was so humiliated that she vowed never to let a boy come near her house again.

Now that she is older and has little contact with her father, Debbie would like to date. But she is more than eighty pounds overweight, and no one ever asks her out. "I try to lose weight," she says, "but food is the only thing I really enjoy. Diets are like torture for me."

Before she left home, Debbie tried several times to commit suicide, each time by cutting herself. Although she has not been suicidal for several years, even today when she feels depressed she experiences strange impulses to cut herself. When you talk with Debbie, it is as if she isn't really there, as if some part of her is in hiding.

If Debbie were married, we might well see the pattern of

sexual abuse repeated in her family. A striking percentage of adults who were sexually abused as children either become molesters themselves or else marry someone who will molest their own children.

The pain that comes from being a victim of childhood sexual abuse is typically buried deep in the heart. It must be uncovered and acknowledged, and in most cases some kind of professional treatment must be sought if the inner wounds are to be healed—and if the intergenerational cycle is to be broken.

Additional Losses from the Molesting Father

1. Because his or her personal boundaries were violated, the sexually abused person may have a hard time setting any kind of limits.
2. The child may veer into promiscuity or, alternately, into an attempt to eliminate sexuality from life altogether.
3. He or she may set out to develop artificial boundaries, such as obesity or isolation.
4. He or she may carry the pattern of sexual abuse into the next generation, in spite of impassioned vows to "never let it happen again."
5. In adult life, the sexually abused person is commonly subject to bouts of serious depression.

The Terrorizing Father

Fathers do not need to physically or sexually abuse their children to create a fear reaction inside them. In counseling, we frequently encounter men and women whose fathers treated them in a way that can only be described as terrorizing them.

Sometimes we meet someone who perceives his or her father as a terrorizer when in fact he was simply trying too hard to be protective. An overprotective father inhibits the development of his children's autonomy and individual identity. In effect, he keeps them children, refusing to lead them out into the larger world because of his own fears. Instead of helping them overcome their fears, he adds his fears to their own.

A true terrorizer, by contrast, is one who severely dominates his children through anger, abuse of power, or overcontrol. The common reaction to having this kind of father is pervasive fearfulness—fear not only of authority figures, but of almost everyone and everything in life. This fear leads to feelings of despair—helplessness and hopelessness. Eventually it turns into depression.

There are three typical but unhealthy ways of dealing with despair. The first is to deny what we feel. When we start to do this as children, we grow up into adults who not only repress bad and painful emotions but are unable to feel *anything,* good or bad, very deeply. We become numb. We may cover up this numbness by overdeveloping our intellectual abilities and defenses, analyzing everything that comes into our field of awareness in order to safeguard our buried emotions.

A second way to deal with despair is to surrender to it and slide into a pattern of weakness and passivity. People who take this course play the victim in every area of life. Moreover, their helplessness actually makes them vulnerable to being taken advantage of by others, which only reinforces the conviction that they are doomed to remain universal victims. Even when they try to create an identity for themselves by becoming caretakers for others, the ones they take care of often take advantage of them, continuing the victimization and perpetuating the fear and passivity.

Victims' behavior in relationships often baffles those around them, who cannot understand why they stay in relationships with people who hurt and abuse them. The tragic fact is that they know of no way to relate to others *except as* victims. To them, being hurt and abused by others is better than being utterly alone.

A third course of action is to acknowledge the despair but to become angry and defiant about it. These are the people who walk around with a chip on their shoulder. Their anger is designed to prevent them from ever being a victim again.

Andy took this third course, the course of anger. He was thirty when he came in for treatment. He had lost his job, and his roommates had kicked him out when he was unable to pay his rent for the third month in a row. He moved back home, but he and his mother were at each other's throat almost constantly. When she told him he must either get help or get out, he called and made an appointment.

Describing his childhood, Andy said, "It was like living in prison, and my father was the warden. I don't remember him doing anything nice for us, ever. If he had a single kind bone in his body, we never saw any evidence of it."

Andy went on to describe a man who, though he never physically beat up his son, was quick with verbal abuse and a smack to the side of the head. "I was terrified of him," Andy said. "When I was little, I used to hide when it was time for him to come home. I never opened my mouth unless I was asked a question. Then when I became a teenager, something snapped. I guess after a couple of fights with some other kids, I realized I wasn't a little boy anymore. I could take on anyone at school. That's when I started to give it back to my dad."

The power struggle between Andy and his father escalated until, when Andy was seventeen, his father kicked him out of the house. Andy quit school and started working.

He had job problems right from the beginning. Interestingly, the jobs he lasted at the longest were those where his boss was like his father—a tyrant. But even with that kind of boss, Andy would sooner or later talk back, or rebel in some other way, and get fired. He has lost count of the number of jobs he had worked over the past thirteen years.

It is clear that Andy's anger is sabotaging his efforts to make it as an adult. His attempts to protect himself wind up being the very things that set him up to repeat the pattern he is trying so hard to avoid. Perhaps he stays with this dysfunctional behavior as a way to mask his underlying depression. Or perhaps he gravitates to tyrant-victim relationships because they are the only kind he knows, the only kind with which he feels comfortable. Perhaps he feels, unconsciously, that even a relationship with a tyrant is better than no relationship at all.

Additional Losses from the Terrorizing Father

1. The child often experiences deep fear that turns into despair.
2. He or she may lead a life of denial in which all emotions are buried.

3. He or she may surrender to helplessness and adopt the identity and lifestyle of a perpetual victim, constantly immersed in fear, guilt, and depression.
4. He or she may become angry and defiant in an attempt to obliterate a deep fear about life.

The Weak Father

It may not seem like it at first glance, but the damage inflicted by extremely weak fathers can be every bit as deep and painful as that inflicted by fathers in the other categories we have been discussing. Usually a weak father will be married to a strong, domineering woman who balances out his passivity and ineffectiveness. This role reversal solves some problems in household management, but it sets up serious confusion in the children's developmental process.

We have spoken of the child's need to go through a process of separation from the mother at age one-and-a-half to two. But how does a child work through separation issues with a domineering mother who has never been a nurturing presence in the first place? Does he simply treat the father as the nurturing parent—the mother figure—and work through these issues with him? That is what usually happens, but the resulting gender confusion is extremely difficult to sort out later.

Rob's family was a classic case. His father was exceptionally weak, and his mother was exceptionally dominant. Her career raising show dogs bordered on being an obsession. Whatever nurturing was done in the family was done by Rob's father; his mother was always too busy raising, training, grooming, and showing her champion Pekingese.

"Dad always said she had a love affair with those animals," Rob said once, "and I guess that was true. The kennel was on the other side of town, and she was there almost all the time. She was never home, it seemed. Of course if it hadn't been the dogs, she probably would have found some other way to avoid us."

Rob's father always deferred to his wife, afraid to confront her about anything. As a result, Rob and his sister, Ann, experienced nurturing as weakness.

"Ann grew up to be just like Mom," Rob said. "She married a guy who's real quiet, who defers to her on everything. They've only been married a year, so I don't know if he'll turn out as weak as my dad—but I wouldn't be surprised if he did."

Rob saw himself as being just like his father. He constantly put himself down for being a wimp. "How am I supposed to be any different?" he would ask. "How am I supposed to be a real man? I never saw any strength or gumption at all in my father. And I hated what I saw in my mother."

Rob's experience is similar to that of a child who loses his father in early adolescence. The main difference is that, instead of giving in to his passivity, he despises himself for what he sees as his weakness. As a result, his depression is closer to the surface, more readily apparent than in the case of mere father absence.

People with exceptionally weak fathers also seem to suffer greater sex-role confusion than do others. They feel they do not have a clue as to what it means to be a man or a woman. The problem for them is not a *missing* role model but a *misleading one*. It is often more difficult to unravel the confusion

184 / *Making Peace with Your Father*

of reversed models than to fill in the gap caused by absent models.

Rob is seriously involved with a young woman, and he worries about the future. "What if she turns out to be like my mother?" he asked. "That would make it almost inevitable that I'd turn out like my dad. But how can I know? Look at my sister—no one thought her husband would turn out to be a wimp, but that's the way it's starting to look. I've got to straighten all this out somehow, figure out what's going on. But how?"

Rob will not find the answers easily. He is, however, asking the right questions.

Additional Losses from the Weak Father

1. The child may experience sex-role confusion.
2. The child may carry over the pattern of weakness into the next generation.
3. Sons often struggle with passivity as adults, leading to depression.
4. Daughters often assume the dominant role by default, at the expense of a balanced femininity.

We have looked at some of the more obvious issues that arise when our father was absent or when his presence was destructive in some way. Bear in mind that there is no way to predict the consequences of a father's absence or dysfunction in the life of any particular child. Many other variables—prominently including the child's personality—enter into the picture. One child might respond quite differently from another, even under very similar circumstances.

One thing, however, is clear: Fathers are essential to the development of both sons and daughters. They are part of the standard equipment of growing up healthy. When Dad is absent or weak or destructive, his children will inevitably be affected.

In these last chapters, we have struggled as we rediscovered our past and felt the pain that resurfaced with the memories. We wrestled with our hurts and our anger as we realized the impact our father's absence, destructiveness, or imperfections may have had in our lives. Now, our natural response is to demand that "Daddy fix it." But that is seldom possible. If in fact he is the cause of our problems, he will, almost by definition, be incapable of correcting the damage he has done.

That means it's up to us. It is we who must confront and deal with the painful issues resulting from what he did or failed to do. Whatever the particular situation we face, it is *we* who must take steps to make peace with our father. In the remaining chapters of this book, we'll begin to discover hope and healing.

Part Four

Hope and Healing

You will know the truth,
and the truth will set you free.
John 8:32

TEN

Facing the Truth

W hy should I even think about my father anymore? He hurt me years ago—and I've spent most of those years trying to forget about him. Why dredge up the past?"

The speaker could easily be any of the people we have met in the earlier chapters of this book. It could easily be you, too. It's a valid question: Why not leave the past in the past?

Even those of us who ask this question most emphatically are often aware that there is something we missed out on back there somewhere, something we are trying to recapture in the present. Although we sense the loss, we are in no hurry to resurrect the pain. In the words of psychiatrist David Hart, we are reluctant to "face the unacceptable." He puts it like this:

Many people fear that if they face the unacceptable, they will *become* it. The exact reverse is true. If you do not face it, you become it. It will always be lived out in one way or another....

The turning point comes when something in us decides that the unacceptable is really meant for us, and we begin to look for its meaning.

If, on the other hand, we employ our usual means not to face what is meant for us—and each of us has his own particular escapes—the terror of the unacceptable not only remains with us, but is also always being lived out as a real disturbance in our lives. We then need constant reassurance that "it is not really so," a precarious and unreal base on which to live.[1]

For many years I was one of those people who refuse to "face the unacceptable." My father died when I was twenty-two years old. My response to his death was to put him on a pedestal, to idealize him. I conveniently overlooked the fact that I had experienced him as an emotionally absent figure for most of my life. More accurately, I pushed that fact into the background. It wasn't something I wanted to remember or think about, so I didn't.

I had a lot of grand ideas about the kind of father I was going to be when I had kids of my own. But when those kids came along and I actually was a father, I found I had little preparation for the job and little realistic basis for my confident assertions about how I would handle it.

Perhaps it was my frustration with not being the kind of father I wanted to be that started reminding me of the fear I had felt as a boy when my father lost his temper. Try as I might, I couldn't push those memories aside. Gradually a flood of old feelings—hurt, disappointment, frustration—came to the surface. My idealized father was gone. Now I had to deal with reality.

The problem with trying to keep our fathers in the past is that the unresolved past is never really in the past. It constantly intrudes into the present, seeking some way to express itself in the here and now. I found myself starting to act like my father in areas where I had sworn I would *never* do things the way he did them. For one thing, I was largely absent from my family because of my work and my schooling. These seemed to me to be good reasons—"excused absences," so to speak—but absences just the same. Only when I started to understand how my early experiences with my father affected me was I able to resolve the past and put it solidly in the past, where it belonged. Until I did that, it kept tripping me up in the present, as if it were trying to get my attention.

So where do we begin? In this chapter I want to outline the first part of a process by which we can begin to make peace with our father. Gaining *understanding* is the first priority.

A woman on a radio call-in show once told me that she had feelings of fear in relation to another person but didn't know why. She wondered if she could work through the process of forgiving the person without knowing what he had done to her.

"I'm afraid not," I told her. "There's really no way to solve a problem without knowing what the problem is."

That lady's question reflects a desire common to many of us: We would like to be able to resolve our "father issues" quickly, easily and painlessly. Sadly, this is seldom possible. The biblical prophet Jeremiah points out that "you can't heal a wound by saying it's not there!" (Jeremiah 6:14). We must be able to identify our problems clearly if we are going to be able to resolve them effectively.

(One important note, however: If your father posed a serious threat of danger to you, and especially if he still does, it is important that you set some limits on your contact with him while you work on these steps. If he is in a position to continue to threaten you or practice destructive or abusive behavior toward you, it will be impossible for you to feel emotionally safe enough to work through this process. Establish some clear boundaries and, if you can, find someone to support you and pray for you.)

Step One: Identify the Symptoms

The psalmist prayed, "Search me, O God, and know my heart; test my thoughts. Point out anything you find in me that makes you sad, and lead me along the path of everlasting life" (Psalm 139:23-24). We usually think that this verse refers to a search for hidden sin—things we have done wrong but have not recognized or acknowledged. Actually there are two types of sin that affect us: the sins we have committed, and the sins that have been committed against us. The two types interact with one another, and both need to be clearly faced and dealt with.

Scripture and psychology are clear on the importance of taking responsibility for what we ourselves have done wrong. At the same time, it is important to recognize that often the sins committed against us, especially when we were children, are the ones that most greatly affect our behavior, our view of ourselves, and the way we relate to others—even as adults.

It may be easy for us to see this in others, but it can be very difficult to see it in ourselves. We tend to back away from looking at the sins committed against us, lest we be thought of as complainers or blamers. Indeed, it is dangerous to shift onto other people responsibility that is rightfully ours. The reverse, however, is also true: It is dangerous to continue a pattern of self-blame and self-condemnation for things that are actually not our fault.

This pattern characteristically begins in childhood, when

we tend to believe that we are personally responsible for everything bad that happens; that if we had only done things differently, or had simply been better, the bad things would not
have happened. Searching out our own wrongdoing is important, but it will not help us resolve the consequences of *other
people's* wrong actions toward us.

As we pray with the psalmist for God to search us and point
out anything within us that grieves him, we can expect that he
will identify whatever prevents us from becoming the person
he created us to be—things we have done, and things others
have done to us.

As I noted earlier with reference to my own experience,
sometimes it is easy for us to identify our symptoms—"where
it hurts"—but it is not so easy to work backward from these
symptoms to the underlying causes. As a father, I found it helpful to look first at the stages when I struggled in my relationship with my sons, and then to look at my relationship with my
own father during those same stages of growth. I also looked
at my problems with authority figures as an indicator of where
I may have experienced father absence. By doing these things,
I was able to identify the symptoms and then work back to the
causes.

Judy is a young woman who experiences a great deal of
difficulty trusting other people. She can open up certain parts
of her life to certain people, trusting this person with one
area and that person with another, but she can't reveal herself completely to anyone. The result is that Judy is a mys-
tery to all her friends. They don't feel they know the real
Judy. And Judy, for her part, never feels confident that there

is anyone she can really count on.

Where does this kind of problem come from? Let's say that Judy's father died in an automobile accident when she was three years old. Today, as an adult, she understands that her father had no control over when he would die. But back then, as a child, Judy felt that her father had abandoned her.

At first Judy's mother depended heavily on Judy for comfort and emotional support. Then her mother began to date someone, and she withdrew emotionally from Judy. That relationship didn't work out, and Mom once again turned to Judy for solace and comfort. This cycle repeated itself several times before Judy's mother finally remarried, when Judy was in high school.

It's not hard to see that Judy's problem with trust has to do with her experience of her mother's erratic way of relating to her: drawing near, then pulling away, again and again. Judy's mother was available to her only when she felt the need for Judy; Judy could never count on Mom's being there for *her*.

We must recognize, though, that in fact *the problem started with the absence of Judy's father*. Fathers play a key role in our ability to trust, in that their presence makes it safe for us to work through our first major developmental task: pulling back from our ties to our mother. Judy blamed her problem on her mother, but she was, in fact, also dealing with an issue of father absence. She was able to identify the symptom, but she needed help tracing it to its real cause.

Another helpful tool in our quest for understanding our symptoms is to consider the men in our lives we have looked upon as "father figures." Who were they? What was it about them that was so appealing to us? The type of father figures we select often helps point us to the particular stage of life at which we experienced father absence.

For example, those who lost their fathers in early childhood will often select father figures who are very nurturing. Those who lost their fathers in later childhood will more likely gravitate toward someone who is a good teacher, someone they are able to learn from—especially about life. Pastors and schoolteachers are often candidates for both these father figure roles.

Sometimes people are drawn to someone as a father figure and then find themselves attracted to that person romantically or sexually. This could be a symptom of father absence in the crucial stage of early adolescence. Not having had a father present when they were discovering their sexuality may lead them to invest relationships with other father figures with sexual overtones.

If we are drawn to father figures who seem primarily to represent wisdom and spirituality, we may simply be trying to "fill in the blanks" resulting from losing our father as adults. We are looking for a spiritual mentor, for the wisdom and guidance that comes with age and life experience.

What about you? I suggest you take a few minutes at this point and skim through the chapters in part 2 where we talked about the consequences of father absence during different stages of childhood development. Do any of those consequences correspond to your own experience? Do any of the stories sound familiar because they describe some important aspect of your life?

In the Step-by-Step Journal at the back of the book, there is an area for you to write out your thoughts as you work through this section. As you finish reading each step, turn to the back of the book and write down your responses to that particular step. Remember, your father doesn't need to have been physically absent for this exercise to apply to you. It may point you to periods in your life when your father, though still alive and living with your family, was relationally detached or emotionally distant from you to some significant degree. Ask God to help you see the things he wants you to see.

Once we have a reasonably clear grasp of our symptoms and of how they might be related to father absence at some point in our past, we are ready to move on to the next step.

Step Two: Get the Facts

There are a number of old sayings about truth. We sometimes say, for example, that "the truth will set you free." That saying comes from the Bible. Other times we say, "The truth hurts." Unfortunately, the second saying is just as true as the first. We all want to be free, but we also recognize that our freedom may come at the cost of accepting some unpleasant truths about ourselves and others. Those who seek freedom while trying to ignore or deny the truth often wind up in another form of bondage instead.

We've already begun our search for truth with a prayer that God will lead us. Jesus promised that the Holy Spirit would "guide [us] into all truth" (John 16:13). With God as our partner, we can be confident in our search, depending on him not only to search our hearts thoroughly, but also to lead us into the truth lovingly and gently.

But didn't we already unearth the truth in the previous step, as we identified our symptoms and traced them back to their causes in our family of origin? Yes and no. It may be more accurate to say that in step one we clarified our *perceptions* of the truth. Now it is time to find out how accurate our perceptions actually are.

The main way to do this, of course, is to talk with other family members. Please note that this does not mean we should go to a sibling or parent and simply unload everything we have been discovering or thinking about. The best way to shut down the entire process of healing is to alienate the very people who can be of most help to us.

A better approach is simply to come to them with an attitude of honest curiosity. Ask questions about different periods of time in your childhood. Take out pictures that you have of yourself as a child, and ask to see pictures that others may have. Look at the expression on your face: What emotions do you see reflected there?

You don't need to do this all at once. Give yourself time. When you try to rush the process, you run the risk of short-circuiting the healing, like when you pick a scab off a wound too soon. Just adopt an attitude of curiosity that makes it natural for you to ask a few questions when opportunities arise.

As you talk with people, compare the new information you receive from them with your own recollections and perceptions and with the understandings you developed during step one. If your understandings and this new information don't agree, don't toss out either one. Most likely you still don't have all the facts. Just let the contradictions lie there for the time being.

If your father is still alive and you are able to have contact, try to spend time with him—but again, only for the purpose

198 / Making Peace with Your Father

of gathering information, not to discuss your feelings or hurts with him. If it feels uncomfortable even to talk with him in this way, take some time to reflect on why this is so. Obviously if he abused you physically, sexually, or even emotionally, you have good reason to bypass this part of the process. Otherwise, ask him about his memory of those days as well as about his own childhood experiences with *his* father. His answers should give you some valuable insights.

If your father has died or cannot be contacted for some other reason, try to contact his siblings—your aunts and uncles. Ask for their memories of your father, and gather whatever information you can about his childhood and adolescence.

Several years ago I was able to travel to Ireland and visit relatives there. During that trip I learned more about the Irish custom that the youngest son cares for the widowed mother, which I had read of earlier in Leon Uris's book *Trinity*. Light bulbs went on in my head. My father had been the youngest son in his family, and his mother had been widowed while he was still living at home. It turned out that he had stayed at home and cared for her until he was thirty-five years old. Only after she passed away was he free to marry. That information helped me gain a new understanding of my father's life.

Once again, understanding is the key. The apostle Paul warned about people who are always learning, "but they never understand the truth" (2 Timothy 3:7). We need to gather facts, but we also need to work at understanding those facts. We need to apply them to ourselves and to our experience of our father.

In my case, learning that my father had spent so much of life caring for a strong, domineering woman helped me understand why it was so difficult for him to share himself emotionally with me. My sister always used to tell me how much Dad cared for me, but I couldn't connect with it; he never showed me his love in ways I could understand at the time. Her insistence that Dad genuinely loved me seemed to contradict my own experience—until I learned more about my father's past.

Of course it often happens that unlocking one riddle only creates new ones. I remember knowing, even as a boy, that my father was a caring person toward other people. I also remember being confused by this: Why couldn't he be that way with me? Now I could see why it was easier and safer for my father to share his feelings with other people. They weren't a threat to him; neither was my sister. But being open with a male was foreign to him. I understood, but I was even angrier now that he couldn't share them with me. Clearly, I was making progress. Equally clearly, I still had a way to go.

As you work at gathering the facts, keep a log of what you are discovering. Make notes about how you experienced your father and the symptoms in your life that might be related to him. Correlate your own impressions with the additional information you are getting about your family, your father, and your relationship to him. You may still be left with some loose ends and some unanswered questions. Don't be concerned: We'll deal with these apparent contradictions in the next step.

Step Three: Identify Family Secrets and Family Myths
Myths and secrets are different sides of the same coin. Secrets are the things that happen that we never talk about; myths are the things we talk about that never happen. Both are untruths,

200 / Making Peace with Your Father

and both tend to contradict the understandings and facts we have established in steps one and two.

The trickiest aspect of confronting secrets and myths is that we ourselves often believe them just as fervently as everyone else in the family does—for the simple reason that we want to believe them. Human nature has a major investment in keeping things the same, and secrets and myths are powerful forces working to preserve the status quo and prevent change.

This propensity for self-delusion goes back a long way. The Bible tells the story of King Ahab and King Jehoshaphat, who were preparing to go to war with the Syrians (see 2 Chronicles 18:5-16). Jehoshaphat suggested they consult the prophets about their plans. Ahab's prophets told him what he wanted to hear: that he would surely be victorious. Jehoshaphat called for a prophet of God, and was given a totally different answer. He warned the king not to go into battle, for he would surely be destroyed. Neither king was willing to take this warning seriously. Each believed what he wanted to believe—with disastrous results. You and I often do the same thing.

Let's talk first about myths. Usually, myths about our father are perpetuated by our mother. Her role often includes serving as the "official interpreter" of Dad to the rest of the family. When he loses his temper, she is usually the one who goes around assuring everyone that he "didn't really mean it," that he really does love us, that the pressures of work or of being out of work, or whatever, account for his reactions. Dad, it seems, never tells us these things himself or even confirms what Mom has said. We believe them partly because it is, after all, our *mother* who is telling us, and partly because we *want* to believe. The alternative is too uncomfortable.

Sometimes our family cherishes myths not just about our father in particular but about men in general. We may be taught that men are big babies, that men can't stand up for themselves, that men are not to be trusted.

Remember the woman I described in chapter 2, who complained that all the men in her family were weak? She may have been correct, of course. But even if she was, does it follow that all the men in the universe are wimps? Of course not. It just looks that way from her perspective. Most likely something in the attraction and selection process used by the women in that family draws them to weak men, and something in the men they are drawn to predisposes them to be submissive to strong, domineering women. The end result is to perpetuate the family myth, which in effect becomes a self-fulfilling prophecy.

One of the best ways to spot a family myth is to observe what happens when a member of the family manages to break away from it. Typically, the person simply gets written out of the family script. For example, if a woman in the family we were just discussing married a strong, capable man, she would likely be ignored by the rest of the family. She and her husband would find themselves left out of family events and seldom even talked about when the family got together. If a son in that family escaped the brainwashing and became a strong male, he would be similarly marginalized—treated, at best, as the exception that proves the rule. Family myths die hard.

Family secrets are often harder to spot than myths, for the obvious reason that no one ever talks about them. They are hidden from view.

I am regularly astonished at some of the things patients turn up while looking for family secrets—not that the facts themselves are so unusual, but that they have been able to stay so thoroughly hidden! I remember a twenty-three-year-old woman named Rose. She was able to discuss her family of origin quite freely except when it came to her father. She simply didn't have much information about him. Imagine her surprise when she did a little probing and discovered that he and her mother had gotten divorced when she was eleven and had never told her about it!

"I knew he wasn't around, of course," Rose said. "But Mom just said he had been transferred to work in a different city and didn't have enough money to come home on weekends. I'd see him about twice a year. Even when he came to visit, he never stayed with us. There was always some reason given, but no one ever really asked about it. I guess we had the impression that we weren't supposed to ask."

Rose learned what had happened through an offhand comment made by one of her cousins. She was livid. When she confronted her mother about the deception, her mother just shrugged her shoulders and said it really wasn't any of Rose's business.

When Rose was finally able to talk to her father about it, he broke down and wept. "I wanted to tell you," he said, "but your mother insisted I shouldn't. As the years went by, it was just easier to keep up the charade."

This rather extreme example illustrates one of the telltale signs of family secrets: a set inexplicable goings-on that everyone somehow "just knows" not to ask about. Secrets grow stronger over time, too—the longer a secret kept, the harder it is to face the prospect confessing to the deception.

Typically, if you start asking questions about areas that appear to be family secrets, you will run into a wall of silence and evasion. When you do, don't press; it won't do any good. Instead, try to find someone who is close to the family but not a family member, and ask him or her. Or talk to the person in your family who has always been ostracized as the "black sheep." Often the person got that label because he or she refused to play along with family secrets or family myths.

There is another category of family secret that is important to note: the kind that is well known within the family but carefully kept from outsiders. Such families often speak of "family business," and the importance of keeping family business "in the family." But an interesting thing happens: These families don't even discuss the "family business" among themselves. The secrets may be known, but they still remain unspoken.

What are some of the myths and secrets in your family? What are the things that everyone talks about as if they were true, but in fact they are not true?

"Dad is too busy."

"That's just the way men are."

"He didn't really mean it."

"I do it because I love you."

Take a few minutes to write down some of the things that were said to you while you were growing up about your father or about men in general. How many of these do you now see to be untrue? Think especially about things that your mother said: These will often be the strongest myths of all. At the same time, take careful note of anything you may have learned about your family, and about your father in particular, that you never knew before, especially those things that were clearly kept hidden from you.

Incidentally, it is important to involve a third party in this process if at all possible—someone outside your family of origin and preferably outside your current family as well. The main reason, as we noted earlier, is that it is hard for us to be objective about these things. Trusted friends can often ask probing questions that help us see things more clearly. They can also encourage us to keep going when we are discouraged about what we are discovering or anxious about what we may discover next.

Now look back at the loose ends and contradictions you came up with in step two. Are there any you can now resolve because you see that they are related to family myths or family secrets?

Step Four: Speak the Unspoken

"Why dredge up the past?" That was the question with which we began this chapter. It's a common enough reaction to the kinds of issues we've been dealing with. In fact, however, this reaction represents a powerful unspoken rule: that these kinds of issues are not to be talked about. It is the very kind of thinking that gives family myths and family secrets so much of their power.

To the degree that what you have unearthed so far about your father and your relationship with him has been painful, it will be easy for you to give up the quest. Why dredge up the past? Why, indeed?

It is amazing how talking with someone else can help us process the pain. Earlier I recommended that you enlist the aid of a trusted friend, someone you could bounce things off as you went about the task of sorting out your recollections and gathering information. Now is the time to share with this person how you are *feeling* about what you are discovering: fear, anger, guilt, shame. These powerful emotions are a natural part of the healing process, but they need to be acknowledged and expressed.

As you become more comfortable talking about your father issues, it is time to share them with someone in your family of origin. Begin with the person you feel safest with. Go slowly. Take your time. See whether the person is going to listen sympathetically or attack you for "daring to say such things about Dad."

Many people's initial impulse is to go straight to the person who has hurt them—in this case, Dad—and confront him, letting the chips fall where they may. That is seldom a helpful approach to dealing with the kinds of issues we are talking about. Often fathers are very skilled at putting the onus back on us; that, after all, is the pattern that developed in our childhood.

"You shouldn't say those things."

"You always asked for too much."

"You're just trying to blame me for your problems."

"It didn't happen."

The fact is, we are not ready to do any direct confronting at this point. We are still gathering information and validating our feelings. It's helpful to get that validation from a family member if possible. If not, we need to simply step back and continue to talk to our support person. The most important thing is that we speak the unspeakable, that we find some way

206 / *Making Peace with Your Father*

to bring out into the light what has until now been buried in the depths of our heart.

Step Five: Rewrite History

To this point we have been working on understanding as accurately as possible what happened to us in relation to our father while we were growing up. We have also been trying to remember how we felt about it. Now it is time to start coming to grips with what didn't happen, to take stock of what we missed out on.

One good way to do this is to write the story of our family life *as we believe it should have been,* or at least as we think it could have been had our father been there for us. How would we like our childhood to have been? What do we wish we had received from or experienced with our father?

For example, Betty lost her father when she was ten years old. The suddenness of it was such a shock to her that she never really grieved over him—she didn't even know how to begin. From that point on she idealized him, remaking him into the perfect father of her dreams. In our discussions, it was impossible for Betty to identify anything he had ever done, or failed to do, that disappointed her in any way.

At one point I asked Betty if she ever felt angry with her father for dying. "That's ridiculous," she snapped at me. "He didn't die on purpose. How could I be angry with him?"

I finally suggested that we talk about the things she had missed out on since the age of ten because of her father's absence—things she wouldn't have missed had he been there. She thought for several minutes. She started to say, "I really can't think of anything . . ." when tears suddenly formed in her eyes.

There was another pause while she collected herself "I haven't thought about this for years," she said, "but I can feel it now as if it happened yesterday. One of my first dates was a formal dance, and I was all dressed up in this beautiful gown. My mom said, 'If only your father could see you now. He'd be so proud.' I started sobbing when she said that, and it took me an hour to get myself together to go on the date."

I suggested to Betty that she make a list of other things she wished she could have shared with her father. Over the next several weeks, we talked about the items on her list, things Betty wished could have happened with her father that didn't happen because he wasn't there. What she was doing was describing her losses.

It is difficult to exaggerate the importance of this in the grieving process. We cannot mourn losses until we understand clearly what we have lost. Rewriting our history helps us define losses. It helps us clarify what we wish we could have had. It even helps us understand what we wish we could experience today. When we rewrite our history, we come to grips with the specific consequences of father absence in our own life.

Another way to do this step is to write a description of the kind of father you wish you'd had. In chapter 3, we discussed the roles that fathers play at different stages of our development. Take some time now to look back over that chapter, and then describe in as much detail as possible what a good father would have been like in your life.

Several years after my father died, I did something I was particularly proud of. I remember thinking, *I wonder what he would think of that? I* wished he could be there, and I wished he would notice and affirm me. I then thought, *Since he isn't here anymore, why not just assume that if he were here, he would say what I wish he would say?* In doing this, I was rewriting my father and his relationship with me. This not only was freeing to me; it also helped me identify what I missed with him and what I needed to do with my own sons.

Here is still another way to get at this issue of identifying our losses. Ask yourself whom you have met who is similar to the ideal father you have just described. Perhaps it is a teacher, or an uncle, or a close friend of the family. Sometimes putting flesh and blood on your ideal father in this way helps make more concrete the impact of your father's absence or inadequacy.

Whichever approach you adopt to this step, write down the results in the Step-by-Step Journal in this book or in your own notebook so you can more readily correlate them with the results of the other steps.

Step Six: Process the Losses
You may have wondered why it was so important that Betty feel her anger at her father because of his dying. Processing anger is an important part of the grieving process. By helping Betty get in touch with the anger that was in fact present in her, though buried deep in her heart, I was trying to help her get back on track with that process. I also helped Betty see that the point was not to *blame* her father for dying, but simply to recognize that her anger was a valid and necessary response to what had happened, one that she should not repress.

To a large extent, making peace with our father is a matter of working our way through the grieving process.

Grieving is the way we adapt to loss. I see grieving as having four stages. The first stage is always denial, which is the refusal to believe such a thing can happen. We are shocked into disbelief. At the other end of the grieving process is acceptance. At this point, we have come to terms with our loss, and to the best of our ability, we have accepted what has happened.

In between denial and acceptance are two major emotions we must process—anger and sadness. As we come out of the protective shell of denial, we encounter intense emotional pain. When we are grieving the loss of a father, we will likely experience feelings of helplessness, separation anxiety—even if it is separation from a father who was really there only in our imagination—and despair. Anger accompanies these intense feelings of helplessness. Often what we feel is so intense as to be almost overwhelming.

One way we cope with these overwhelming feelings is to blame ourselves. A child may try to make bargains in her mind, thinking that if only she had been better behaved, more obedient or more helpful around the house, then Daddy would have changed his mind and not gone away. Even after the father leaves, the child will often continue to blame herself, trying to behave better in the hope that Daddy will come back home.

The other core emotion of grief is sadness. This is often experienced as depression, and it follows close behind our self-blaming. Here are the tears over the reality of our loss. These two emotions—anger and sadness—don't come in any order. During our grieving, we will often move back and forth between them, noticing only that the intensity begins to lessen over time.

What I've noticed over the years is that women seem to have no problem expressing the sadness in grief, but have trouble focusing the anger outside of themselves. Men seem to have no problem expressing the angry part of grieving, but struggle with letting themselves experience the tears and the sadness. Studies have shown that when this occurs, the person gets stuck in the grieving process, leaving him or her unable to move into the place of acceptance. When we hold on to our anger, either by keeping it focused on ourselves, or by repressing it, it settles into our hearts as bitterness and resentment. When we hold on to our sadness, we end up stuck in depression. Either way, we stop ourselves in the middle of the healing process, unable to let go of our pain and to experience freedom.

My father died years before I began dealing with my issues in relation to him. In some ways, his being gone made the process easier. As I worked through my anger and my grief, I was able to feel my feelings without having to deal directly with him. The downside was that, not being able to deal directly with him, I could not experience potentially positive changes in our relationship. Whether your father is dead or alive, some things in this process will be easier for you, and others will be more difficult. Either way, the task is yours. You need to work on it for yourself.

Betty had experienced the denial and the sadness. But she felt she could not let herself feel anger at her father for dying. It just didn't make logical sense to her. Once she saw that anger was a normal part of the grieving process, and once she let herself experience and express her anger, she was finally able to get unstuck and move on to the fourth stage of grieving, acceptance. She experienced what the psalmist described: "Weeping may go on all night, but in the morning there is joy" (Psalm 30:5).

Now that you have arrived at a clearer notion of what you have lost because of your father's absence from your life, you are in a position to work through the grieving process. Bear in mind that grieving has a rhythm of its own. We cannot force it to happen. But we can encourage it to happen by our willingness to work through our losses one step at a time.

Take some time to reflect on how you have handled your grief in the past. What was damaged or destroyed by your father's absence or abuse? In what ways have you denied your losses? How have you been able to express your anger over these losses? What kinds of bargains did you make in your mind, hoping to recapture what you felt was missing? How did you handle your feelings of helplessness? You may find it helpful to write down the answers to these questions. Also, don't forget to talk through what you are experiencing with your trusted friend. It will help keep the grieving process moving forward.

The information we have learned about fathers and the six steps we have just taken make up the first half of our journey toward reconciliation with Dad. So far, we have been journeying inward as we have learned about fathers in general and our father in particular.

Now we will begin the journey outward. We will look at what we can actually do about our losses now that we have come to grips with them, and we will take hold of whatever may still be available to us in our relationship with our father.

ELEVEN

Making Peace with Your Father

T he six steps we discussed in the last chapter were designed to help us clarify the issues we need to deal with in our loss of our father. They represented, we said, a journey inward, gathering information about what happened to us and then understanding how we have been affected by those events. Now it is time to start the journey outward. In this chapter we will look at five steps to completing the grieving process and making peace with our father.

Step Seven: Wait

For many of us, our first inclination once we have come to grips with our situation is to run right out and start setting things straight. Often, this "don't just sit there, do something" approach makes things even worse—as Susan discovered.

Susan's father, while not a terrorizer, was nevertheless quite controlling. His combination of powerful authority and emotional distance made him a formidable presence in Susan's life. Not surprisingly, Susan's relationship with her father was always quite strained. They seldom spoke to each other except in family gatherings.

Now, however, Susan had a full head of steam. She called her father on the phone and without any warning or preparation, let him have it with both barrels.

Susan had been meeting with a group of other people who were also working on their father issues. At their next session, several days later, Susan was still shaken from the experience of calling her father.

"I told him, all right," she said. "I mean really told him. Everything. At least until the point where he hung up on me. That was bad enough. But the worst part was when my mother called me. She was practically hysterical. She said if that was the way I was going to be then I could consider myself no longer part of the family."

Susan was sobbing as she recounted her mother's reaction. "I can handle *his* rejection," she said. "I mean, he's never been there for me anyway. But my mom! I can't stand the thought of hurting her."

Rather than experiencing healing and freedom, Susan had only made her problem worse.

What many of us tend to forget in our eagerness to pursue healing is just how long we have lived under our negative circumstances. It has been only very recently that we have gotten on top of the situation. All our life we have viewed our father as a *parent,* as an authority figure, as someone who was probably beyond our understanding and certainly beyond our capacity to judge. Only recently have we been able to look at him as a fellow adult.

The fact is, it takes time for us to assimilate all the new information we have discovered and to internalize the new understandings we have developed. We spent years internalizing the *old* understandings and patterns of relating. We owe it to ourselves to take time to internalize the new ones as well.

Otherwise we are like a basketball team that has been trailing a tough opponent the entire game and then takes the lead in the closing minutes. It's not time to celebrate victory just yet—let alone to start taunting our opponent. There is still time left on the clock. The game isn't over yet.

Obviously there is no way to specify precisely how long this waiting period should last. One helpful principle is that we should wait at least until our strong impulses or urgency are past—until we feel confident that we can take the next steps peacefully and with self-control. As a general rule, the earlier the loss or injury occurred, the longer the recovery time will need to be. By the same token, the more severe the injury was, the longer it will take to heal. A serious violation of our personal boundaries early in childhood will require a longer waiting period than a less serious problem that occurred in late adolescence.

Even during this time while we are not actively working on our problems, we will nevertheless begin to experience changes. Typically we will find that we are starting to respond differently to people around us. Where once we were passive, we may find ourselves taking more initiative, risking our vulnerability with people in ways we never would have dared before. Where once we were angry and defiant toward authority, we may find our attitude softening. These subtle changes will be noticeable not only to us, but also to those around us— as Joan found out.

Joan was in the same group as Susan, and she had been thinking of taking a similar course of action. At the last minute, for some reason, she thought better of it. After listening to Susan's story, she was glad she waited. She resolved to be patient and to give herself all the time she needed before taking the next step.

Over the next weeks and months, Joan began to share with the group that she was growing irritated with several of her close friends. When she described her frustrations, one of the men in the group pointed out some of the ways in which Joan herself had been changing.

"You seem more confident, and you're becoming much more direct in your communication," he said. "Do you think that maybe your friends don't like some of the changes you're going through?"

Joan thought for a moment and then said, "Maybe so. I *do* find that I feel different when I'm with them—maybe I am acting different, too. And now that you mention it, I find myself spending time now with a different crowd—people I used to avoid because I always felt intimidated by them. Now it just seems to me that they're . . . I don't know, *healthier* than my old friends, somehow."

I pointed out that this is a very common experience among people who are working on these kinds of issues. Not that we necessarily drop our old friends—though that may happen. But we change, and the changes in us affect our relationships. Joan was using the waiting phase to practice new relational skills with her friends, and some of them didn't know what to make of it. I suggested she share with a few of her friends some of what she was going through, in hopes that they would be able to understand and accept the changes in her.

For Joan, the waiting phase is a time of becoming stronger. Eventually, when the time comes to work things out with her father, she will be able to do it from a position of strength, not from anger or desperation. It is the same for all of us. A waiting phase gives us time to grow stronger, to develop inner confidence that will help us take the remaining steps.

Step Eight: Forgive

I can already hear your reaction: "Forgive! Are you kidding? *Forgive* my father for what he did to me? Don't you understand how badly I've been hurt?"

It's understandable that we feel that way. Especially as we become clearer on exactly what we lost in our relationship with our father, our tendency is to desire *justice*. We want to get even. God understands this desire, and he promises to satisfy it: "He gives justice to the fatherless" (Deuteronomy 10:18). The important thing is that we let God be the one to pursue justice on our behalf, not try to take it into our own hands. At this point in the process, our part is to forgive.

Myths of forgiveness. Our resistance to the prospect of forgiving someone who has hurt us—in this case, our father—is often related to some common misconceptions we may have about forgiveness.[1]

For example, many times we resist forgiving someone because we believe that by doing so we will condone bad behavior.

We often verbalize forgiveness by saying, "That's okay. It was no big deal. Forget about it." But when someone has wounded us deeply, everything in us cries out that it is *not* okay, that it *is* a big deal, and that the last thing we want is simply to dismiss it as though it never happened.

Forgiveness, however, does not mean condoning bad

behavior or pretending nothing ever happened. In the Bible, Paul describes it as canceling a debt (see Colossians 2:13-14). This is like what a bank does when it cancels a debt that it knows is unpayable; banks even call it "forgiving" the debt.

The bank does not act as though the debt never existed or as if the debtor's inability to pay it were "no big deal." If that same person were to come back and ask for another loan, you can bet the bank would scrutinize his or her credit records carefully—and, in all probability, say no. Yes, the debt was forgiven. But not paying it back was definitely not okay, and there are still consequences to be borne. When we forgive our father, we are not saying that the injuries he caused us never happened or that what he did was okay.

It is clear from Scripture that when God forgives us, he is definitely not saying that it is now all right for us to go on sinning. That is never part of the equation. Sin is serious. It cost God a great deal—the life of his only Son—to cancel the debt of our sin. Although he is glad to cancel it, he never intends for us to conclude that it is now okay for us to go out and sin some more. In the same way, our forgiveness of our father in no way condones what he did or endorses his doing it again. It simply cancels the debt from the past.

Another misunderstanding about forgiveness is that it is the same as *reconciliation*. Actually, while forgiveness and reconciliation are related, they are still two separate processes. Forgiveness is unilateral: It is something I can do all by myself. Reconciliation is bilateral: It is something both parties must do together. If you have hurt me, and we are estranged as a result, I can forgive you on my own, without your permission, without your even knowing about it. But we are not reconciled until we sit down and take mutual action together.

In terms of our fathers, one of our ultimate goals may be to achieve complete reconciliation. Although that is the ideal outcome, it is not always possible. Our father may be dead. He may still pose a danger to our well-being so that we cannot approach him for reconciliation. He may simply be unwilling to reconcile. *This does not, however, mean we cannot forgive him.* Forgiveness is something we do on our own initiative with or without his cooperation. There will be time later to explore the possibility of reconciliation. For now, the task is to forgive.

A third misconception about forgiveness is that it is a *quick, simple process.* Let's say, for example, that you and I are walking together and you accidentally step on my foot. You say, "Oh, I'm sorry," and I say, "That's okay. I forgive you." It seems so superficial. How can anyone expect us to casually brush off the kind of hurt that our father's absence or abuse has caused us?

The answer, of course, is that we are *not* expected to brush it off casually. In fact, that kind of quick, superficial interaction often is not really forgiveness at all—it is merely *excusing* what has happened. Genuine forgiveness is something much deeper, much more powerful, and much more lasting than simply excusing wrong behavior.

A fourth misconception about forgiveness is that in order to forgive, we must forget. If we still retain the memory of what was done to us, we think, then we have not truly forgiven. In fact, just the opposite is true: To forgive is to *remember.* That is because forgiveness is not just a one-time action on our part; it is usually something that we must choose to do over and over again. If we are to continue to forgive, we must continue to remember.

The confusion on this point usually arises because God has told us that when he forgives us, he remembers our sins no more (see Isaiah 43:25). What this means is that God no longer relates to us on the basis of our sins—he puts them out of his mind when he thinks about us. Besides, God can afford to forget about our sins because he does not need to learn anything by remembering. We, however, often need to be able to remember what has been done to us, because we can learn valuable lessons from our experience.

What happens when a child burns herself touching a hot stove? Should she "just forget about it"? On the one hand, yes—we wouldn't want her to go through life paralyzed by the fear of burning herself every time she turns around. On the other hand, however, she needs to remember the experience so she can properly be on her guard in the future. So it is with us. We need to remember the harmful things that have been done to us, not so we can wallow in them, not so we can let them dominate our life, but so we can learn from them and avoid repeating them.

Genuine forgiveness. So far we've talked about what forgiveness is not. But what *is* it? How does it work?

Think back to our example of the bank forgiving a debt. This is not an arbitrary action on the bank's part, not something that "just happens." It is the result of a deliberate decision. The bank officers carefully evaluate the situation. Can the debtor possibly repay the loan? Is it worth making any further effort to collect what is due? Only when they are persuaded that the answer to all these questions is no do the officers take the step of canceling the debt.

This is just what we do with regard to our father. In the first six steps, we assessed the hurt and damage he caused us by his absence or abuse. In effect, we totaled up our losses. During the waiting phase, we gave our emotions time to settle down so that we can make a clearheaded decision about what to do next. In time we come to this inevitable conclusion: Dad can never be the father we needed him to be.

This is true for two reasons. First, most of our losses were sustained in the past, and no one can go back and change the past. The losses we sustained in childhood are in this sense irrecoverable.

But what about the present? Or the future? Can Dad be the kind of father we need him to be today? Or tomorrow? Does he have the resources, the capability? Perhaps you can already see that the answer to these questions must also be no. The second reason Dad can never be the father we need is that no *human father can ever be perfect.* And when you get right down to it, the perfect father is what all of us are seeking, even if we haven't articulated it that way.

The only perfect father, however, is our Father in heaven. Our earthly father can never measure up completely. Thus no matter how we calculate our losses, no matter how we reckon the amount that our father owes us for our pain and difficulty, we will always arrive at the same inescapable conclusion: He can never pay us back.

Once we understand this, we have three options. We can repress our awareness of it—try to pretend it's not true. We can acknowledge it, but with bitterness and anger. Or we can accept it and take the only course of action that offers us hope of healing and freedom. If our aim is truly to make peace with our father and to move on in a life of joyful wholeness, *we have no choice but to forgive him.*

Remember, forgiveness is something we do as the result of a considered decision. The banker in our illustration may not want to forgive the person who owes him money. It may be costly for him to accept the loss. But once he realizes that it is necessary and unavoidable, he takes the step. And that is that.

How do we know when *we* are ready to take this step? We know we are ready to forgive our father for the hurts of the past when we are able to be comfortable expecting little or nothing from him in the present and in the future. I don't mean by this that we should become cold and cynical in our attitude toward him. I simply mean that as long as we are cling-ing to the hope that he will someday succeed at being the kind of father we really need—as long as we are expecting him to do the impossible—then we are setting ourselves up to be dis-appointed. If we hang on to this vain hope, it is usually a sign that we have not yet finished mourning our losses.

When the time comes—when you feel confident that you are ready—make the decision to forgive. Talk with God about your decision. Ask him for the strength to follow through on it. Then mark your decision in some symbolic way.

Do something concrete to symbolize the fact that you have taken the step of forgiveness. The future will likely bring some painful reminders of past hurts. At such times it is helpful to have a tangible token of the fact that the debt has been can-celed.

For example, if you have been keeping a notebook during this whole process, you may want to go through it and write the word *canceled* across each page in big letters. Some people burn their notebooks or bury them. If you haven't kept a journal or notebook, you may want to write a letter to your father stating your losses—and then tear up the letter. Simply talking things through with your trusted friend may be sufficient.

If your father is dead or otherwise unavailable to you, you may want to "talk it through" with him anyway. One woman I know went to her father's grave and spoke her forgiveness to him just as though he were there with her. Other people do the same thing with a photograph or even an empty chair.

The fact that he is not really there isn't important, since for most of us, the father we need to forgive is the father we have internalized in our memories and imaginations. We simply need to find a way to make the transaction concrete, so that in the future we can look back and say, "On this date, in this place, I cancelled the debt against my father."

Step Nine: Invite Others to Share Your Journey
Only after we have completed the step of forgiveness are we ready to take the step of confrontation: to go to our father and tell him what we have been discovering about our life and about his role in it. If we reverse the order—if we confront before we have forgiven—we will inevitably carry expectations that will leave us vulnerable to disappointment and further pain.

The purpose of confrontation is not to blame, unload our negative emotions, punish or get even. To many people, confrontation implies hateful words and acrimonious accusations. This kind of angry scene—sometimes called "parent-bashing" by those unlucky enough to have been on the receiving end— is usually counterproductive. When we are through, the only thing anyone remembers is our anger—not the substance of what we had to say.

The purpose of confrontation is to help bring healing and peace to ourselves and to others. It may or may not bring about reconciliation, but that is not the main point. The main point is to invite our father, as well as other members of our family, to join us in our journey of healing and recovery. David Augsburger calls this approach "care-fronting."[2]

Remember Joan, the young woman who decided to wait awhile before confronting her father? Let's pick up her story again. Joan's father abandoned her, her mother, and her two brothers when Joan was six years old. After the divorce, he moved across the country. Although he was faithful about sending his monthly child-support checks, he never came back to visit Joan or her brothers. Nor were any children ever invited to go and visit him. They talked on the phone occasionally for the first several years. Then even that contact was broken off.

After identifying and acknowledging her feelings and grieving for what she has lost, Joan has finally come to the point where she is ready to forgive her father. She shared with her support group what she did.

"I took my journal and read it through one last time," she said. "It was really emotional—at one point I thought I might never stop crying! Then I wrapped the journal in brown paper, taped it shut, and tied a string around it. I wrote the word *forgiven* across the front and back."

She paused for a moment, as if anticipating what some of the group were thinking. "I thought about destroying it," she said. "But I put a lot of work into that journal, and I wanted to keep it. Still, I wanted it sealed shut. Anyway, as far as I'm concerned, it's over now."

As the group talked with Joan about what to do next, it seemed that the best course of action would be to share her experience with her mother and brothers before approaching her father. Talking openly with her mother would be difficult. "My role with Mom was always to protect her emotionally," Joan said, "so going to her with my pain won't be easy."

The group helped Joan devise a way to invite her mother to share in the process she had been going through without placing blame on her. Sharing with her brothers would be easier; she had already been talking with one of them about what she was experiencing.

Each of these invitations to share her journey was really a sort of dress rehearsal for her intended visit to her father. Talking with her mother and brothers helped her clarify what she wanted to say and how she wanted to say it. She hasn't set a date for meeting her father yet, but she is putting together a plan for how the process will work. She has an old high school friend who lives about fifty miles from her father's home; she will schedule a visit with this friend and stay at her house. That last part is important for Joan. It gives her confidence to know she has a safe haven to go to if the visit with her father doesn't go well.

The group probed carefully to determine Joan's motive in confronting her father. "I don't really have any expectations as far as his response is concerned," she said. "Whether he takes it well or not doesn't matter to me. There's just a part of me that wants him to know how his leaving affected me. Until I started working on these issues, I never knew whether I loved my dad or hated him. Now I can see it's a bit of both, and I want him to at least hear that from me." Joan is acting according to a principle expressed by King Solomon: "Open rebuke is better than hidden love" (Proverbs 27:5). Often an important component of our own search for truth is the ability to speak the truth plainly.

Dan is in his late twenties. He hadn't heard from his father since he was seven years old. His mother spent most of his childhood years belittling his father whenever the subject came up. She eventually remarried, and Dan's stepfather agreed that contact with his birth father would not be good for Dan. It took a lot of effort for Dan to work through his feelings of loss as well as his fears about what he would find if he ever reestablished contact with his father.

Finally, through a relative, Dan was able to track down his father's address. He wrote a short letter to his father just to test the waters. When he got a brief but cordial note in response, Dan decided to seek his father out. With a business trip to a nearby city coming up, he was able to schedule some extra time for a side visit to his father.

"It was incredible," he told me. "I mean, just hearing the other side of the story after all these years. I still have a hard time thinking of him as my dad. But I really want to get to know him better." Recently Dan invited his father to go on a camping trip with him—as if to recapture some of the lost moments of childhood.

Each confrontation is different. Some go very smoothly: The father listens carefully and then tearfully expresses from the heart the sorrow he feels, as well as the loss he has experienced as a result of his absence from his children's lives. In other cases, the father just sits there in silence as if he doesn't know what to say. Still other fathers get angry, defending themselves and shifting the blame to the mother or to someone or something else. When this happens, it is best to end the conversation quickly, offering to talk more if Dad is ever interested in doing so.

Dan's is a wonderful success story. It sounds so simple. Yet it was able to take place only after Dan had done a lot of emotional spade work. The camping trip with his father didn't just come out of the blue; it came only after Dan carefully worked through all the preceding steps. Had it gone badly, he would have been prepared to handle it.

You may decide not to make contact with your lost or estranged father for various reasons. It may simply not be possible. That is okay. Face-to-face confrontation is not a required part of the process. Many people find that the emotional confrontation involved in identifying their feelings, calculating their losses, and writing a journal during their healing process serves the same purpose. In any case, what is most important is not what happens between us and any other individual; what is most important is what happens inside us.

Step Ten: Explore New Roles

At this point, we have essentially made peace with our father. We have worked through a process of self-discovery and self-understanding. We have arrived at a point where, having totaled up our losses, we are able to cancel the debt our father owes us. We have decided whom, if anyone—including our father—we wish to invite to share this journey with us. Now we are finally able to consider what kind of relationship we may be able to have with our father, both in the present and in the future.

It is important to recognize that *we* are the key person in this step. More than any other factor, the choices we make will determine what kind of relationship we will have with our father. Having acknowledged our pain and anger, having dealt with it and set it aside, we will likely find ourselves ahead of other family members—including our father—in our emotional growth. As such, *we* become the key person in stopping the intergenerational cycle of sin and hurt that may have plagued our family. *We* become the pacesetter. The changes that have occurred in us will be the foundation on which our entire family can build.

An interesting thing often happens inside people once they finally put their father issues to rest: All of a sudden, they feel grown-up. Often when I speak to various groups about these issues, I ask the people to remember the last time they were with their parents. Then I ask them how old they felt inside at that time. The answers typically range anywhere from six to sixteen. Very few report that they feel like adults when they are with their parents.

By dealing with our father issues, we free ourselves to finish growing up emotionally. We look back on a recent trip back home and realize that for the first time we didn't feel like a kid anymore in our father's house.

We may also notice the same phenomenon occurring in other situations, in our relationships with other adults. I remember years ago when I was an associate pastor on a church staff, sitting around a conference table at the church's executive board meeting and thinking, *What on earth am I doing here?* I felt like a youngster who had wandered into the wrong room by mistake. Looking back, I wonder how many of the other board members—many of whom were my age—felt the same way.

Some time later when I was sitting with another group of men and women, my mind flashed back to those earlier church board meetings. I realized there was a striking difference between the way I was feeling now and the way I felt then. Then I felt like a child among grown-ups; now I felt like an adult among my peers. What had happened? Well, I had added a few years to my life; that probably helped some. And I had completed my training as a psychologist, in the meantime, which also probably helped a little. But it was during those intervening years that I came to grips with my father issues—that I worked my way through essentially the same steps I have described in this book. That was what made the biggest difference.

It is a pattern I have seen repeated time after time, in other people's lives. Most people begin to notice these changes during the waiting period—step seven. At that stage we begin experimenting with our new feelings and practicing our new skills with friends and acquaintances. When we start to apply them within our family, we really notice the changes taking hold. First we deal with our father issues. We learn to think about and relate to him in a new way. Then we are able to grow up in relation to our mother and siblings, our spouse and children. From there, our newfound emotional adulthood spreads rapidly through our other relationships.

A note of caution: Not all the negative symptoms of father absence simply disappear. We still have some work ahead of us. But be encouraged; we are now able to go about that work effectively and fruitfully. As we practice being the adult person we have become, we will feel stronger, more comfortable around other adults, and more capable of dealing with our struggles.

Step Eleven: Redeem the Past

We are often tempted, as we see more clearly what we may have lost or suffered because of our father's absence or abuse, to view all those early years as wasted. We look at the pain and wonder what purpose it served. What meaning can it have for us now? It all seems so useless.

In reality, nothing could be further from the truth. God has a purpose for everything that happens to us. Every experience—positive or negative—ultimately takes its meaning from the way God uses it in our life.

This is not the same as saying that God is the direct *cause* of everything that happens. Sometimes people explain their negative experiences by saying, "God did it to me to teach me a lesson." That is backward. God is in the redemption business. He takes the bad things that happen to us because we live in a fallen, sinful world and turns them to our good. When we blame God for our problems, we miss out on the ways God is trying to redeem them and use them for our benefit. That is what the apostle Paul meant when he wrote, "We know that all that happens to us is working for our good if we love God and are fitting into his plans" (Romans 8:28). Another translation puts it more directly: "Everything that happens fits into a pattern for good" (Phillips).

I recently had the chance to ask Dan how he feels today about the pain he experienced when his father abandoned him and about the resulting losses he has sustained. "It was difficult to go through it all," he said. "I'm a better man for it, though. I wish it could have been different. But then I wonder how I ever would have experienced the growth that's come to me as a result of facing my father issues."

No normal person really welcomes pain, I suppose. At some level, however, all of us realize the truth of the familiar slogan *No pain, no gain.* It is only by grappling with challenges and trials that we come to maturity. Even those who have had to recover from the effects of a raging tyrant of a father, or a father who abused or molested them, can eventually look back over the process of healing and realize that God has brought something good out of their pain.

Not long ago at a weekend conference my wife and I met a woman who shared with us her painful story of being molested by her father when she was young. "I struggled for years with my secret," she said. "I only wish I had known sooner what resources were out there to help me." She then told us how she had started a nonprofit resource network for those going through the nightmare she had experienced.

"Hardly a day goes by," she said, "that I don't talk to eight or ten people who were victims of physical abuse, sexual abuse, even ritual abuse. I spend six to eight hours a day researching various agencies and then letting people know how to get in touch with them. I send out lists of books, hotline numbers, support groups, and events people might want to attend. It has been an important part of my healing." It has also been an important way that God has redeemed her pain, using her to reach out to others as no one else could do.

Not everyone needs to start a hotline or a resource network. Some may simply be able to talk quietly with one person at a time, providing support and strength for healing. Others may find different ways to redeem their past and serve as messengers of hope. Ask God to show you how he wants to redeem *your* pain by using you to promote the healing of others.

TWELVE

God Our Healing Father

When anthropologist Margaret Mead said that father-ing was nothing more than a social invention, she was expressing a belief shared by many modern people. Mothering seems purely instinctual; fathering does not. To many people there seems to be nothing inherently necessary about fatherhood beyond the initial act of procreation.

But as we have seen in this book, that view of fathering is wrong. The father is every bit as important to the child's devel-opment as the mother. God designed both parents to play integral roles. God himself is our source of understanding of what fatherhood is all about.

If we have mistaken understandings of fatherhood, we have an even more distorted understanding of God our Father. I have deliberately left this chapter until last, not because it is of least importance, but because my experience has been that people are not ready to internalize the truth about God's fatherhood until they have sorted through their issues with their earthly father. Then scales seem to fall from their eyes, and they are suddenly able to see God as a true Father.

Many, perhaps most, of our ideas about God come from what we see and experience in the natural realm with our earthly father. When that relationship is flawed—as it in-evitably is—we tend to project those flaws onto God, assuming (often without thinking about it, or even realizing that we are doing it) that he must be like our father in these respects.

For example, people raised by a tyrannical father often picture God as an angry despot who always expects too much. The Bible even lends support to this view; the Old Testament in particular often seems to depict a God who is harsh and demanding toward his people and even worse toward his enemies. If our father was a tyrant, we may hear people speak of a loving and gracious God, but we see no sign of him. We tremble at the thought of God (as we have pictured him), just as we used to tremble at the thought of our earthly father.

Or we may struggle with an image of an aloof, distant God. This was the case with me. I remember in my youth saying that as far as I was concerned, God always seemed to be "a day late and a dollar short." I didn't realize I was projecting onto God my experience with my natural father, who usually was either too busy or too tired to be involved with me. I think part of my motivation for becoming a minister was the belief that in full-time Christian work I might find the closeness with God that I had always heard about but never experienced. It was only after I mourned my losses from my father that I became able to experience intimacy with God.

In my counseling work through the years, I have met innumerable people who feel deep anger toward God. Invariably, as I help them explore their relationships with their family of origin, I find that they also harbor strong anger toward their father. Usually they deny that there is any connection. Nevertheless, we nearly always discover that in truth their anger toward God is connected with their anger toward their father. The behaviors they attribute to God are precisely the behaviors they experienced growing up.

We must be very clear about the relationship between human fatherhood and the fatherhood of God. Human fatherhood is not the pattern for divine fatherhood. Just the opposite is true. Divine fatherhood came first; it is to be the model for human fatherhood, not the other way around. When we project our human experience of fatherhood onto God, we are pointing the projector in the wrong direction! We need to begin with what the Bible says about God and then take that as our model for human fatherhood.

What *does* the Bible tell us about God? We have already noted that people with negative images of God, if they are from a churchgoing background, often seem able to find scriptural support for their picture of what God is like. Does the Bible really present this kind of distorted image of God? No. Only when we select isolated passages are we able to make the Bible "prove" that our images are accurate. When we stand back and look at the Bible as a whole, a more complete and balanced picture emerges. We've already noted how God models for us the four fathering roles. Let's look at two more aspects of God's character as a Father.

God Our Patient Father

The parable of the Prodigal Son, with which we are all so familiar, should really be called the parable of the patient father. The main point of the parable is to tell us some important truths about God our Father—aspects of his nature that have never been seen in any earthly father. When Jesus first told this story, the love and forgiveness expressed by the father were almost totally incomprehensible to his listeners.

According to Jewish custom, a son could receive his share of his inheritance prior to his father's death if the father wished to give it to him. The father might, for example, want to turn his affairs over to his son so he could retire. But the parable presents us with a brash young man who heartlessly demands his share right now. The father wisely does not argue with his son. He realizes the boy will have to learn things the hard way. He grants his son's request without lecturing him or heaping on guilt.

Eventually the father's worst fears come true. His son fails miserably; ending up doing something Jews were forbidden to do—feeding swine. Then, at his lowest point, the son comes to his senses and decides to return home, planning to ask if he can be accepted as a hired hand in his father's household.

The father has been longing for this very moment, the moment when his son would hit bottom and come back to him. While he gave his son the freedom to leave, he never let his son leave his heart. He allowed his son to fail, never trying to rescue him as so many well-intentioned human parents do. This father knew how to practice tough love. His stance was firm even as his heart was soft. And all the while, he waited patiently and persistently.

Then comes the moment he is longing for. While the son is still a long distance away, his father sees him coming and runs out to meet him. Before his son can even finish his rehearsed speech of repentance, his father interrupts him and calls for the servants to bring him the finest robe, a ring for his finger, and shoes for his feet. Scripture commentator William Barclay says that "the robe stands for honor; the ring stands for authority, for if a man gave to another his signet ring it was the same as giving him the power of attorney; the shoes stand for a son as opposed to a slave."[1]

The father cancels the debt his son owes. He keeps no record of the son's failure and sin. Even though there certainly are negative consequences for the son—his inheritance is lost—this is not held over his head as a "lesson" for the future. The father simply accepts his repentance and welcomes him back into the family. He even proclaims a feast to celebrate the joyous occasion!

Most of us have heard this story many times. Hopefully as we hear it again we will once more feel wonder and awe at the great love this father shows for his child—because it is precisely the kind of love that God our Father has for us. Our God is a Father who doesn't keep score. He doesn't punish us for selfish reasons. He doesn't turn away from us when we struggle or suffer. When we work through our painful experiences with our earthly father, our heavenly Father stands beside us, weeping when we weep, rejoicing when we look to him to restore our losses—as only he can do.

The son in the parable sins willfully and deliberately. So do we. Yet God's grace and forgiveness toward us always remain intact. He cannot stop loving us! "For I am convinced," Paul says, "that nothing can ever separate us from [God's] love. Death can't, and life can't. The angels won't, and all the powers of hell itself cannot keep God's love away. Our fears for today, our worries about tomorrow, or where we are—high above the sky, or in the deepest ocean—nothing will ever be able to separate us from the love of God" (Romans 9:38-39).

That pretty much covers it all, doesn't it? If we have been abandoned or abused or damaged in some other way by our earthly father, those words of assurance and Jesus' story of the patient father remind us what God our Father is like—and how is so much more than our experience of our earthly father.

God Our Healing Father

God specializes in healing broken hearts. Isaiah wrote of God's Messiah, "The Lord has anointed me to bring good news to the suffering and afflicted. He has sent me to comfort the brokenhearted, to announce liberty to captives, and to open the eyes of the blind" (Isaiah 61:1). When he announced the beginning of his ministry at the synagogue in Nazareth, Jesus took these words to himself. In so doing, he showed us God's loving, compassionate heart.

David also assures us that "the Lord is close to those whose hearts are breaking" (Psalm 34:18). He adds in another place that God "heals the brokenhearted, binding up their wounds" (Psalm 147:3).

God knows our pain, our loss, our disappointments. He longs to heal our brokenness. He could do so instantly—but then we would not learn the lessons that are vital to our healing. For most of us, his promise to heal our broken hearts will be fulfilled over a period of time.

The writer of the letter to the Hebrews assures that "this High Priest of ours understands our weaknesses. . . . So let us come boldly to the very throne of God and stay there to receive his mercy and to find grace to help us in our times of need" (Hebrews 4:15-16). We can stay there as long as we need to in order to experience the fullness of God's healing grace.

As you work through the process of healing described in

this book, invite your loving heavenly Father into the process with you. Allow him to heal your shame and guilt. Bathe each step you take in prayer. Ask God to empower you to follow through on each step and to endure the pain and hurt you experience. Ask him for the courage to risk making changes, both in your behavior and in your expectations. Ask him to give you the grace to forgive, so that you may be released from the bondage of the past.

Then ask him to give *you* the robe of honor, the ring of authority, and the shoes of a beloved son or daughter. Let God show himself to you as the Father to the fatherless.

He has already made peace with you. He is waiting for you to come home.

A Step-by-Step Journal for Making Peace with Your Father

Making peace with Dad is our objective, but many of us never quite get started unless we have a step-by-step guide through the process—especially since facing the truth about him is not always pleasant or easy.

In the chapters of this book, we have looked at some suggestions for this process. But here are some more detailed steps you can take in working through this process in your relationship with your father.

Feel free either to write in this book or to keep a separate notebook. Either way, *it is important that you write out your responses.* Something about writing things down makes the process work better.

Step One
Identify the Symptoms

We have identified some of the symptoms you might experience as result of your relationship with your father. Let's look more closely at what happened.

Describe, as best you can remember, your relationship with your father in the years before you went to school.

_____

_____

_____

Describe that relationship while you were in elementary school.

_____

_____

_____

Describe your relationship with your father during your adolescence.

_____

_____

_____

What is that relationship like today?

_____

_____

_____

How do you think your relationship with your father—or your lack of relationship—has affected you?

_____

_____

_____

How is it still affecting you?

_____

_____

_____

How do you deal with your anger?

_____

_____

_____

In what ways are you passive? Do you tend to be passive, or are you passive only occasionally?

_____

_____

_____

Do you sometimes feel overwhelmed? When? In what circumstances?

_____

_____

_____

What are some ways your attitude toward anger could be related to your relationship with your father?

_____

_____

_____

Describe your father in terms of the father roles listed below, noting how he did and did not fulfill each role in his relationship with you.

The Nurturer
Ways my father nurtured me

_____

_____

_____

Aspects of the nurturer that were missing in my father

_____

_____

_____

The Lawgiver
Ways my father was a lawgiver in our family

_____

_____

_____

Aspects of the lawgiver that were missing in my father

_____

_____

_____

The Warrior/Protector

Ways my father protected me

_____

_____

_____

Aspects of the warrior/protector that were missing in my father

_____

_____

_____

The Spiritual Mentor

Ways my father was a spiritual mentor to me

_____

_____

_____

Aspects of the spiritual mentor that were missing in my father

_____

_____

_____

Using the previous pages as a springboard, take some time and make two lists. In the column on the left, list things you can identify from part 3, "When Father Let Us Down," that might be issues for you. Then, in the column on the right, list the ways your father let you down.

246 / *Making Peace with Your Father*

Things I Struggle With	*Ways My Father Let Me Down*
_____	_____
_____	_____
_____	_____
_____	_____
_____	_____
_____	_____

Step Two
Get the Facts

When you have completed step one, you have a picture of how you experienced your father. Step two checks the accuracy of your perceptions. To do this, you need to talk with other family members. At this point, all you are doing is seeking information.

Whom can you talk to in order to get additional information about your father? List all the people that are still living that you can contact. Be sure to talk to any person identified in your family as the "black sheep"—black sheep are often exceptionally honest about the family history. If you are short of family members, what about some of your father's friends? (In Ireland I found an octogenarian who played with my father when they were boys.) Who might you find that knew your father when he was young? Use the following lines to list all the family members and friends you can think of.

_____

_____

_____

_____

_____

_____

_____

_____

As you talk with these people, how does what they tell you change the image you have of your father?

_____

_____

_____

As you talk with your father's family and friends, you may find descriptions of him that contradict or contrast with your experience of him. List the contradictions you are finding.

_____

_____

_____

What questions about your father are still unanswered? What gaps are still in your understanding?

_____

_____

_____

Step Three
Identify Family Secrets and Family Myths

Gaps in our understanding of Dad may indicate family myths or family secrets. Myths are the things we talk about in our family that never really happened. Secrets are the things that happened in our families that we never talked about. Read over pages 199 to 204 and think of your own family situation. What might be some of the myths in your family? List them.

_____

_____

_____

_____

What might be some of the secrets in your family? List them.

_____

_____

_____

_____

Take your list of myths and secrets to a trusted friend who has known you for a long time and who also knows your family, if possible. Talk with your friend about each list, point by point. Look back at the last two questions on page 247. Now that you have identified and discussed some of the family myths and secrets, are there any contradictions or loose ends that you can resolve? How are these contradictions resolved?

_____

_____

_____

_____

_____

_____

Step Four
Speak the Unspoken

This step does not involve confrontation. Here you are attempting to speak to *yourself* the truth about your feelings about the past. Often these feelings seem negative. Some of them may feel quite overwhelming. That's why it's important to talk about these emotions with someone you trust. But first you must get them down on paper.

What are you feeling as you look more at the truth about your father? Finish these sentences:

I feel *angry* about _____

I feel *guilty* about _____

I feel *afraid* of _____

I feel *ashamed* of _____

I am *sad* about _____

I feel *betrayed* by _____

I feel *abandoned* because _____

I feel *helpless* when _____

I feel *humiliated* by _____

I feel _____ about _____

I feel _____about _____

I feel _____about _____

I feel _____about _____

Now take what you have written and share it with your trusted friend. Your friend's task is to listen, to question, to clarify, and to validate your emotions—that is, to help you recognize and accept your true feelings.

Step Five
Rewrite History

This important step helps us to identify what *didn't* happen that we wish had happened. It helps us to take stock of what we have missed out on. Let your imagination loose and invent the family life you wish you had.

What kind of father do you wish you had? Describe him as best you can.

_____

_____

_____

What are some things you wish your father had done with you that he didn't?

_____

_____

_____

What are some things he did that you wish he hadn't done?

_____

_____

_____

If you had the power to make it happen, what do you wish your father would say to you today?

_____

_____

_____

Whom have you met who is close to your ideal of what a father should be like? Describe what makes him seem that way to you.

_____

_____

_____

Step Six
Process the Losses

In step five you identified the things you have lost in your relationship with your father. Whenever we experience loss, we need to grieve.

252 / *Making Peace with Your Father*

The first element of grieving is *denial.* We aren't ready to face the truth.

A big part of grieving is acknowledging the anger we feel at having lost something important. We direct some anger *outward* at other people. We turn some anger into *bargaining*—trying to change the situation. We channel some anger *inward* at ourselves and become depressed.

The final element of grieving is acceptance.

Denial
Describe how you have denied your issues with your father.

_____

_____

_____

Anger Directed Outward
What kinds of things are you angry about?

_____

_____

_____

With whom are you angry?

       Your father

       Your mother

       God

       Life

       Your family of origin

       Someone or something else

Describe your feelings of anger.

_____

_____

_____

Bargaining

When you were a child, how did you think you might influence the way your father acted? What kinds of bargains did you try to make? List as many as you can remember here:

_____

_____

_____

If only I . . .

_____

_____

_____

then maybe my father would . . .

_____

_____

_____

Look back on what you have written. Notice how much responsibility your bargaining thoughts placed on you. Write yourself a disclaimer—a note releasing yourself from that responsibility.

_____

_____

_____

Anger Directed Inward

Depression is anger turned upon yourself. In what ways have you been angry with yourself in regards to your relationship with your father? If you're having trouble getting started, jot down what comes to mind when you hear the words *fail* or *fear*. Or ask your trusted friend to help your brainstorm.

Don't forget to talk through with a trusted friend what you are writing.

_____

_____

_____

_____

_____

_____

Step Seven
Wait

This is an important phase. It keeps us from reacting too quickly to our newfound emotions of hurt and anger.

It is important to wait, but it is also important to "do something." This is the time to expand and develop our support group.

List the names of the people you trust the most, the ones you will draw around you as your support team.

_____

_____

_____

Who are some other people that might be supportive to you in this process?

_____

_____

_____

How will you meet with these people? Will you start a support group? Will you meet for lunch on a regular basis? Describe your plan to develop your support system.

Where we will meet:

_____

_____

_____

When we will meet:

_____

_____

_____

How often we will meet:

_____

_____

_____

How we will remember to meet:

_____

_____

_____

List some people you know (*family members, friends, people on your support team lists*) who don't feel completely safe. Could you work on and develop your relationship with some of the people on this list? If so, put an asterisk by their names.

_____

_____

_____

List some people who are not safe at all.

_____

_____

_____

Describe how you will protect yourself in your relationship with the people who are not safe at all.

_____

_____

_____

Step Eight
Forgive

We've already looked at the process of forgiveness in chapter 10. We described forgiveness as "canceling a debt." List or describe the "debt" owed to you by your father. What should he have done for you that he did not do?

_____

_____

_____

Is there any way your father can repay this debt?

_____

_____

_____

Given what our father owes us and his inability to pay us back, we have three options for dealing with this "debt." We can repress it, pretending it isn't there. We can nurse it into bitterness, dwelling on the injustice. Or we can forgive it by canceling it, knowing the debt is unpayable. Which is your choice?

If this choice is difficult for you, perhaps you need more time to process your losses and grieve. Go back and spend more time on steps six and seven.

When you feel ready, write the word FORGIVEN across the "debts" you listed on the previous page. Then live free of the burden.

Step Nine
Invite Others to Share Your Journey

This step goes beyond confrontation. It is an invitation to other family members to share your journey with you. It may also include your father, if that seems like an option.

List below the family members you want to share your journey with. Place a number by each name to rank them in order, from the easiest person to invite to the most difficult and scary person to invite.

_____

_____

_____

Outline what you want to share with these people about the process you have been going through.

_____

_____

_____

Describe the time and place you will begin this process, starting with the easiest person on your list and moving through the list in order from easiest to scariest.

Person's Name   *Time*   *Place*

_____

_____

_____

After you share with the first person on your list, write out some of your reactions to that meeting.

_____

_____

_____

What did you learn?

_____

_____

_____

What should you not do in the future?

_____

_____

_____

What was the best part of your sharing together?

_____

_____

_____

Do the same for the second person on your list.

What did you learn?

_____

_____

What should you not do in the future?

_____

_____

_____

What was the best part of your sharing together?

_____

_____

_____

Write down any other important things you learned as you shared your journey with people on your list.

_____

_____

_____

Step Ten
Explore New Roles

As you complete the first nine steps, you make peace with your father *within yourself.* You have also brought other significant people into your process with you, perhaps even talking to your father about what you have worked through in your emotions.

Now comes the step where you will change the way you relate to your father today, as well as how you relate with other significant adults in your life.

To begin this step, look back at step five, where you rewrote your history. In that process, you stated a number of things about how you wished your relationship with your father could have been. Restate what you wrote in step five in terms of today.

How would you like your relationship with your father to be today?

_____

_____

_____

Describe how *you* want to act in that relationship today.

_____

_____

_____

Many times we describe what we want, even though we know that some of our ideals may never be realized. Evaluate what you have written in the last two pages about your relationship with your father. Which things are possible to change? Which things may never change?

Things That Might Be Changed

_____

_____

_____

Things That May Never Change

_____

_____

_____

Describe now one or two things that you will do differently the next time you are with your father.

_____

_____

_____

Step Eleven
Redeem the Past

In chapter 10, we talked about how God can redeem even a painful, damaging relationship with our fathers. He can use our hurt in some meaningful way in our lives today. Before planning how God might use your past to help others, take a look at what you have learned through this process. Write down as many things as you can think of that have been meaningful to you in the process of making peace with your father.

Who might benefit from your sharing with them what you have experienced?

Write a letter of thanks to God and to those who walked with you in this healing process.

Notes

ONE
The Journey Toward Dad

1. Sulivan, "Working Dads Pose Problem," *Dallas Morning News,* June 12, 1991. Dad will be almost entirely absent from the scene.
2. Guy Corneau, *Absent Fathers, Lost Sons* (Boston: Shambhala, 1991), 11-12.
3. Sullivan, "Working Dads."
4. Based on information gathered by the National Center for Fathering, 217 Southwind Place, Manhattan, Kansas 66502.
5. National Center for Fathering, Kansas.

TWO
What Only Dad Could Do

1. Margaret S. Mahler, Fred Pine, and Anni Bergman, *The Psychological Birth of the Human Infant* (New York: Basic Books, 1975).

THREE
The Four Roles of Fathers

1. Rick Fields, *The Code of the Warrior* (New York: Harper Perennial, 1991), 265.
2. Gary Smalley and John Trent, *The Blessing* (Nashville, Tenn.: Thomas Nelson Publishers, 1986), 24.

FOUR
God as Our Model for Fatherhood

1. C. F. D Moule, *The Holy Spirit* (London: Mowbrays, 1978), 29.

FIVE
Father Absence in Early Childhood

1. Joseph Nicolosi, Ph.D., *Reparative Therapy of Male Homosexuality* (Northvale, N.J.: Jason Aronson, Inc., 1991), 44.

SIX
Father Absence in the Elementary School Years

1. Leon I. Hammer, "Female Sexuality," in *Modern Woman: Her Psychology and Sexuality,* eds. George Goldman and Donald Milman (Springfield, Ill.: Charles C. Thomas), 182.

SEVEN
Father Absence in Adolescence

1. Peter Blos, *Son and Father* (New York: The Free Press, 1985), 12.

TEN
Facing the Truth

1. David Hart, "The Path to Wholeness," *Psychological Perspective* (Fall 1972), 152.

ELEVEN
Making Peace with Your Father

1. For a more detailed discussion of the myths of forgiveness, see David Stoop, *Forgiving Our Parents, Forgiving Ourselves* (Ann Arbor, Mich.: Servant Publications, 1991).
2. David Augsburger, *Caring Enough to Confront* (Ventura, Calif.: Regal Books, 1974). If we are able to confront with an attitude of caring about those involved, we will greatly enhance our chances of being heard.

TWELVE
God Our Healing Father

1. William Barclay, *The Gospel of Luke* (Edinburgh: St. Andrew's Press, 1953), 212.